Britain's Buses in a New Era
The Opportunities and Threats Ahead

BUS INDUSTRY MONITOR

A Passenger Transport Monitor publication
Independent Analysis & Commentary since
1991

Published by Passenger Transport Intelligence Services Limited

83 Latimer Road, Eastbourne
East Sussex BN22 7EL
e-mail: info@passtrans.co.uk
Web: www.passtrans.co.uk

ISBN 978-1-898758-21-1

© Passenger Transport Intelligence Services Limited 2024

All rights reserved. No part of this publication may be used, reproduced or transmitted in any form by any means electronic or mechanical, including the photocopying, recording or by an information storage and retrieval system, without prior permission in writing from the publisher.

Author: **Chris Cheek BA FCILT MCMI**

Contents

Preface 6
Editorial Comment 8
Part A: Where We've Come From 16
1. The Market since 2010 16
    1.1   Operator Income 16
    1.2   Changes in Service Levels 21
    1.3   Changes in Passenger Numbers 22
    1.4   Fares: The DfT Fares Indices 24
    1.5   Revenue Yields 27
2. Bus Operating Costs 29
    2.1   The Overall Picture 29
    2.2   The Structure of Bus Industry Costs 30
    2.3   The Importance of Labour Costs 30
    2.4   The Importance of Time and Speed 31
3. The Need for Profit 33
    3.1   Why is profit necessary? 33
    3.2   Sustainable Profits 36
    3.3   Profits under a Franchised Regime 37
    3.4   Use of Operating Leases 37
    3.5   Key Conclusions 38
    3.6   Actual Performance 38

Part B: Bus Regulation 42
4. The National Bus Strategy and BSIPs 44
    4.1   Introduction 44
    4.2   BSIP Delivery and Regulation 44
    4.3   First Round Funding 45
    4.4   Covid and BSIP+ 45
    4.5   Individual Allocations 45
5. Enhanced Partnerships in England 46
    5.1   Overview 46
    5.2   The EP Plan 46
    5.3   The EP Scheme(s) 48
    5.4   Local Authority Obligations 49
    5.5   Bus Operator Obligations 49
    5.6   Governance Arrangements 50
    5.7   Operator Objections 50
    5.8   Consultation 50

5.9	EPs and Competition Law	51
5.10	Criticisms of the EP Process	52

6. Bus Service Improvement Partnerships in Scotland 54

6.1	Origins and Legislation	54
6.2	The BSIP Plan	54
6.3	BSIP Partnership Scheme	54
6.4	Bus Operator Obligations	56

7. Bus Franchising 57

7.1	Introduction	57
7.2	An International Perspective	58
7.3	Franchise Architecture	63
7.4	Implementation	66
7.5	The Tyne & Wear Experience	69
7.6	CMA Guidance	70

8. Local Authority Ownership 71

8.1	Historical Context	71
8.2	The Current Position	71
8.3	Routes to New Municipal Companies	72
8.4	The Local Authority Ownership Debate	72

Part C: The Key Tasks Ahead 74

9. Improving Performance 75

9.1	Driver Recruitment	75
9.2	Traffic Congestion and Bus Priority	76

10. Increasing Service Levels 78

10.1	Introduction	78
10.2	Reasons for the Increases	78
10.3	Achieving Increases	78
10.4	Paying for Services	79
10.5	Patronage Expectations	79
10.6	How Much it Might Cost	79

11. Decarbonising the Fleet 84

11.1	Overview	84
11.2	Vehicle Costs	84
11.3	Infrastructure	85
11.4	Government Funding Assistance	85
11.5	Quantifying the Costs	86
11.6	Repowering	88

12. Net Zero and Modal Shift 90

12.1	The Historic Context	90

12.2	The First Targets	91
12.3	The Blair Government's Response	91
12.4	A Change of Emphasis	92
12.5	The Current Targets	94
12.6	Transport Decarbonisation Plan	94
12.7	What the Targets Might Mean	95
12.8	Modal Shift Targets in Scotland	98
12.9	Modal Shift Targets in Wales	99

Appendix A: Sustainable Profits – A Worked Example 100

Appendix B: Bus Speeds – A Worked Example 113

Appendix C: BSIP Funding Allocations 116

Appendix D: Rural-Urban Classifications 122

Appendix E: Sector Financial Performance 124

Index of Tables

Table 1: Bus Industry Income	20
Table 2: Bus Kilometres Run	21
Table 3: Urban/Rural Split in Kilometres Run	22
Table 4: Commercial/Supported Proportions of Bus Kilometres	22
Table 5: Bus Patronage by Type of Passenger	24
Table 6: Bus Patronage by Urban/Rural Split	24
Table 7: Passenger Revenue Yields, 2009/10 v 2022/23	27
Table 8: Bus Operating Costs by Sector	29
Table 9: Fleet Size and Average Age, 2009/10 v 2022/23	34
Table 10: Local Bus Service Earnings, 2010-2023, GB Outside London	39
Table 11: Local Bus Operating Margins by Sector, 2009/10 v 2022/23	40
Table 12: Levels of Planning and Control in Public Transport	59
Table 13: Surviving Municipal Bus Operations in Great Britain	72
Table 14: Resource Implications of Extending the Operating Day by 1 hour	80
Table 15: Restoring Services to 2019 Levels in GB Outside London	81
Table 16: Restoring Services to 2010 Levels in GB Outside London	82
Table 17: Restoring Supported Services to 2010 Levels	83
Table 18: Fleet Replacement Needs, 2023	87
Table 19: Fleet Replacement Requirements by Year	87
Table 20: Estimation of Market Potential for Repowering	89
Table 21: Demand for Travel by Mode in GB – Summary Table	93
Table 22: Estimated Bus Demand Gains from Modal Switch	97
Table 23: Travel Demand and Mode Share in Scotland, 2022/23	98
Table 24: Travel Demand and Mode Share in Wales, 2022/23	99

Index of Figures

Figure A: Breakdown of Ongoing Industry Income, 2009/10 and 2022/23	19
Figure B: Real-Term Changes in Bus Fare Levels since 2009/10	25
Figure C: Quarterly Bus Fares Index since 03/2019: England	26
Figure D: Quarterly Bus Fares Index since 03/2019: Scotland, Wales & GB	26

Figure E: Revenue Yields per Passenger Kilometre by Sector 28
Figure F: Bus Industry Cost Structure, February 2024, GB Outside London 30
Figure G: The Bus Industry's Vicious Circle 32
Figure H: The Need for Profits in the Bus Industry – the ARCC Analysis 37
Figure I: Local Bus Operating Margins, 2010-2023, GB Outside London 40
Figure J: Professor Gwilliam's Bus Regulatory Cycle 43
Figure K: The Enhanced Partnership Process 48
Figure L: Bus Service Improvement Partnerships: The Process 55
Figure M: Procedures to Introduce Bus Franchising in England 67
Figure N: Procedures to Introduce Local Bus Franchising in Scotland 69
Figure O: Demand for Travel by Mode, 1952-2022, Great Britain 90
Figure P: Bus & Coach Market Share of Travel Demand since 1992 93
Figure Q: Passenger Journeys by Distance Travelled, England, 2022 96
Figure R: Estimated Passenger Km by Distance Travelled, England, 2022 97

Preface

Welcome to this latest report in our *Bus Industry Monitor* series. This volume focuses on the future of the industry following the change of government in July 2024, setting it in the context of the changes that have taken place since the last Labour government left office in 2010.

I've entitled the report ***Britain's Buses in a New Era*** for several reasons:

- firstly, there is little doubt that the experience of the Covid-19 pandemic and its aftermath fundamentally changed society and the economy and therefore the context in which the bus industry works.

- secondly, because the publication of the National Bus Strategy in March 2021 and its subsequent implementation has created a new era in terms of regulation.

- thirdly – most recently – because the election of a Labour government in the 2024 general election has marked another shift in government approaches to the bus industry and indeed transport policy as a whole.

This report, and its predecessors over the years since we began the *Bus Industry Monitor* project back in 1991, is designed to provide a body of evidence on what is happening on the ground in the industry. As my late colleague Peter Huntley put it in the original introduction to the reports, *"though the industry continues to attract much attention, particularly in the context of developing Government transport policy, much of the opinion expressed is based on generalised statement rather than on objective research."*

It can be argued that Peter's concern, first expressed some 30 years ago, remains valid in some areas, even after all this time. Much more work has been done over the years, but many assertions made about the industry and its structure continue to show limited understanding of the operational and financial realities of delivering a quality bus service.

The evidence we have accumulated over the years has led to us to a deeper understanding of the issues at stake, and hopefully we are able to communicate that through reports such as this one, and our parallel activities.

This latest document builds on our knowledge and adds the latest data and other research, taking the opportunity to update and refine analysis that we have presented before.

The report is divided into three broad sections, looking at:

- the bus market as it has evolved since 2010 (chapters 1 to 3)

- the future of bus regulation (chapters 4 to 8)

- the key tasks ahead (chapters 9 to 12)

In Chapter 1, we review the statistics for income, service levels, patronage and fare levels since 2010, whilst Chapter 2 looks at both the structure and level of costs. We cover the need for profits in Chapter 3, included an updated analysis of target profit levels in the light of current financial circumstances and the need to fund future investment needs.

Turning to regulation in Part B, Chapter 4 reviews the National Bus Strategy and the development of BSIPs, whilst Chapters 5, 6 and 7 examine the various forms of current regulation in more detail, looking at Enhanced Partnerships, Bus Service Improvement Partnerships in Scotland, and Franchising. The latter also considers what international experience can teach us about a competitive tendering regime. Finally in this section, Chapter 8 looks at the question of municipal ownership.

Part C focuses on the future, looking at the four key tasks that the government, LTAs and operators need to deliver over the next few years. These are:

- Improving performance
- Increasing service levels
- Decarbonising the fleet
- Delivering modal shift to help deliver net zero.

In the latter three areas, we present new analysis on the resource implications of increasing service levels, on the cost of decarbonisation and the implications of current modal shift analysis.

Hopefully, this volume will contribute to the aim of widening knowledge of the industry and how it works and will add to that body of objective research which Peter Huntley was so keen to build throughout his career.

The *Bus Industry Monitor* reports are researched and produced by Passenger Transport Intelligence Services Ltd as part of our normal commercial activity and are not funded, supported or assisted financially in any way by any other organisation, authority or group.

Chris Cheek
Passenger Transport Intelligence Services
October 2024

Editorial Comment

Reviewing the Years since 2010

As I have noted before in these reports, determining how to measure success or failure in the bus industry can be quite difficult and the verdicts are usually controversial. In practice, the availability of published and directly comparable data also places limits on what can be used – though much more data is publicly available than in earlier years (at least in England).

There is a widespread hope in the industry that the General Election and the subsequent change of government may mark a new beginning for the bus industry and public transport in general. Thus, this seemed a good point at which to take stock and examine what needs to be done for the future and how much it might cost – but also to understand where the industry has come from. For the lessons of recent history can show us the pitfalls and illustrate the threats which might derail that new beginning.

Unlike previous reports, which have tended to focus on year-on-year movements, this one takes a longer view, looking at the changes that have taken place over the last 14 years. Choosing fiscal year 2009/10 as a starting point for this report seemed apposite for a number of reasons:

- it marked a high point in the industry's fortunes before the effects of the financial crisis took hold
- it marked the point at which political control changed from Labour to the Conservative/Lib Dem coalition
- it marked the commencement of the period of austerity in the public sector, whose effects have been felt throughout the industry ever since.

The first thing to say is that nobody could credibly contend that the industry was in robust health or had achieved either prosperity or market growth since the Labour Party left office in the early summer of 2010.

The measures we have examined, based on our review of statistics and spending data from the DfT and the Scottish and Governments, include:

- Bus industry income
- Bus service levels (kilometres run)
- Numbers of passenger journeys
- Fare levels
- Revenue yields
- Bus industry costs – both levels and cost structure
- Changes in net revenue levels

The information on these subjects is discussed and analysed in more detail in Chapters 1 and 2. In summary, we find that:

- bus industry income outside the capital fell by 24% in real terms during the period, driven by cuts in passenger income (23%), BSOG (50%), supported services (33%) and concessionary fares reimbursement (25%). In London, income fell by 16%
- bus service provision fell by 27.7% across GB outside London between 2009/10 and 2022/23. The cuts in the supported networks were even greater, at 49.8%, and this figure rose to over 60% in some areas of the English Shires. Service levels run commercially by bus operators fell by 20.7%
- passenger volumes fell by almost one-third across Great Britain outside London, whilst the capital lost one fifth of its patronage. Wales saw the biggest drop, with a 47.8% fall, followed by the English Met areas on 34.7% and Scotland on 34.3%
- bus fares across all areas increased ahead of inflation from the start of the period until Covid. At their peak, the fares indices showed real term increases of over 22% in the English Shires, 16% in the Met Areas, 14% in Scotland and 10% in Wales. Since then, the introduction of discounts targeted at certain groups, alongside the £2 fare cap introduced in England, have driven the indices lower – though this may not represent the experience of many passengers
- despite the fare increases for many people, passenger income per passenger kilometre, when adjusted for inflation, has risen by just 4.9%[1].
- Unit cost levels rose in real terms:
  - The per kilometre rate increased by 12.4%
  - Costs per passenger journey have risen by over 30% over the period, compared with growth in income per passenger journey at 9.2%.

Job cuts and fleet reductions followed, with investment postponed, resulting in a marked increase in the average fleet age and the retention of older, more polluting vehicles on the road for longer.

The changes happened for a whole variety of reasons, including:

- a 20% cut in Bus Service Operators' Grant (BSOG), forcing fares up in many areas
- reductions in spending by local authorities, faced with significant budget cuts, who started to reduce supported services and cut the staff who planned them
- growing traffic congestion, slowing bus journey times and making services more expensive to operate
- weak economic performance, with productivity and real wages struggling throughout the decade
- other socio-economic changes, including the growth of online shopping and the loss of high street footfall
- the growth of homeworking, which began to impact on travel demand
- a sustained fall in world oil prices which – coupled with a failure by government to increase fuel duty in line with inflation – saw the pump price of fuel fall by 45% in real terms in four years, making bus travel much less competitive than it had been.

Then came Covid – not only the lockdowns themselves, but their consequences, including

---

[1] *In this context, passenger income includes concessionary fare reimbursement.*

- massive increases in home and hybrid working
- boosts to the move online for shopping, personal business and education
- a significant reduction in the propensity to travel amongst older people.

DfT's weekly statistics on post-Covid travel volumes continue to show passenger volumes below pre-Covid levels[2]. In the fiscal year 2023/24, average levels were 89.1% in both London and the rest of GB – this represented an increase from 2022/23, when the averages stood at 84.4% and 83.0% respectively. At the time of writing, year to date figures for the period April to August 2024 show an average of 89.7% in London and 87.3% in the rest of the country.

Regulation

In the four years since our last report, two major changes have occurred, which will be monitored closely over the next five or ten years:

- The publication and first steps to implement the National Bus Strategy for England (NBS)
- The first introduction of a franchised network, in Greater Manchester.

As we describe in Section B, the process initiated by the publication of the NBS has got into gear, with the development of Enhanced Partnerships in the majority of Local Transport Authority (LTA) areas, followed by the implementation of the first initiatives in those LTA areas that received government funding approval. At the time of writing, it is too soon to be able to say whether these are delivering the improvements and patronage gains envisaged.

The government stated firmly that there would be no return to a post-deregulation model where bus services had been planned on a purely commercial basis with little or no engagement with, or support from, LTAs. This was perhaps a surprising statement in view of all the work that had been done to promote partnership working since 1992 and the earlier legislation on this subject, but well may have been a warning to authorities who had not fully engaged as much as to the bus operators.

The move towards franchising of networks has taken several steps forward. Firstly, the first two stages of Greater Manchester's new franchised network were launched in the autumn of 2023 and the spring of 2024, with the third tranche to be launched in January 2025. Again, it is far too soon to be able to judge the impact of the changes, though Transport for Greater Manchester (TfGM) is reporting some early gains in terms of both patronage and performance.

Elsewhere, the example of TfGM is being followed, firstly by the Liverpool City Region Combined Authority, which is preparing to launch its first stage in 2025. Other Mayoral Combined Authorities are actively considering a similar move, including Cambridgeshire & Peterborough, South Yorkshire, West Yorkshire, Tyne & Wear, West Midlands and the West of England.

In October 2024, it will be 38 years since the implementation of the 1985 Transport Act – the very legislation which provided the impetus for the *Bus Industry Monitor* project in the first place. Since then, there have been very few years which have not seen some form

---

[2] *PTIS analysis of Daily Usage of Transport by Mode: Great Britain, since 1 March 2020, Department for Transport.*

of debate about the future regulation of the industry. Unfortunately, over the years, such discussions have generated much heat and remarkably little light.

Governments of both parties have legislated since the 1985 Act – in 2000, 2008 and 2017 – and in Scotland in 2001 and 2019. Further legislation is promised for Wales at the time of writing. Each reform has been designed to assist the bus industry but has also made provision for the re-regulation of the quantity of services – usually by local transport authorities. Remarkably, it took more than 20 years before anybody implemented those powers.

Meanwhile, further legislative change is promised by the new government, which announced a 'Better Buses Bill' in the King's Speech in July 2024, and announced changes to secondary legislation in September, just as we were going to press. This will make it easier for LTAs other than Mayoral Combined Authorities to introduce franchising if they so wish and simplify the complex process of franchising more generally. This is discussed in Chapter 7 below.

The rest of England, meanwhile, was directed by the Johnson Government towards the Enhanced Partnership regime introduced by the 2017 Act. As can be seen in Chapter 5, this is a complex procedure which nevertheless has the potential to deliver significant improvements to bus services and their operating environment. Some weaknesses have been pointed out, which may be addressed in the promised new legislation.

Chapter 6 looks at the parallel process in Scotland, known (somewhat confusingly) as Bus Service Improvement Partnerships – though progress here is much slower, held back by the even more constrained financial position of the Scottish Government and the suspension of the Bus Partnership Fund.

As we have noted before, though, whatever regulatory reform is eventually delivered can only be an enabling force. What really matters is the delivery of benefits to existing and potential users on the ground. The evidence still shows that these are best delivered by strong local authorities working in partnership with high-quality bus operators.

Ultimately, though, people will not use unreliable, slow, expensive bus services whether they're directed from the town hall or the bus company. And the taxpayer will not pay for inefficient and poorly used services.

Those are the twin lessons which the disastrous period of failure between 1974 and 1986 taught the industry. Meanwhile, the experience of some operators and local authorities over the last few years reminds us that they are still valid today. The financial problems encountered by state-owned bus and rail operators in both parts of Ireland as well as other parts of the world since Covid have been a reminder that public ownership and control is not the panacea that it is sometimes portrayed.

Similarly, local authority ownership of commercial bus operations – offered by some as a way forward for the industry – has at best mixed history, with some notable success stories but also a string of bankruptcies and forced sales – these are discussed further in Chapter 8.

Even in London, for so long rightly held out as a model of success for modern bus operations, a combination of congestion, financial constraints and socio-economic change is prompting a fall in demand and cuts in service provision.

In fact, both tendered and commercial systems are perfectly capable of delivering poor quality and inefficiency. Equally, both can deliver significant improvements – what matters is the partnership and the control of congestion, not the control of supply through regulation. Changing who makes the decisions about network design and how much to charge does not affect the need for operators to work with planners, highway authorities, enforcement agencies and infrastructure providers to deliver high quality bus services.

The industry's critics are fond of pointing to the patronage growth achieved in London and comparing it with continuing decline in the rest of the country. However, as we have argued many times over the years, such comparisons ignore several key differences between the markets, which have determined the different outcomes and will continue to have a decisive influence on future performance. These include underlying market conditions such as population density, car ownership levels, population growth, generous concessionary travel schemes for senior citizens and children, the size of the workforce size, which modelling work demonstrates have a decisive influence[3]. As one consultant put it to me, "The only thing we can learn from London is about London".

Thus, politicians and others who are convinced that London-style regulation will give them London-style trip rates and growth are doomed to disappointment.

Looking to the Future

As so often in the past, we can divide a discussion about the industry's future into two time periods – the near-term, covering perhaps the period up until 2030, and the longer term, from say 2030 to 2050 – already the focus of much attention because of the Net Zero targets.

Not for the first time, it is difficult to be optimistic about the short-term prospects. there is funding uncertainty about BSIPs and Enhanced Partnerships, whilst other funding problems threaten existing levels of service, especially in those areas where BSIPs were not funded by DfT.

The longer term can look very promising, but it is extremely difficult to see how to get from one to the other – especially when the risk of further short-term damage could make the longer term transformation even more difficult to achieve.

Future outcomes will be heavily influenced by how well and how quickly the industry and its partners can deliver on the four key tasks we identified in the Preface, namely:

- Improving performance
- Increasing service levels
- Decarbonising the fleet
- Delivering modal shift to help deliver net zero targets.

The four are inextricably linked: successful delivery of the first three tasks would be essential if there were to be any chance of delivering the modal shift. We believe that all four will require significant additional funding.

Performance Improvement

Performance improvement can only be delivered by investment in better infrastructure to give buses priority and improve the journey experience and by the ability to recruit and retain the right calibre of front-line staff.

---

[3] *See for example our publication The Bus Demand Jigsaw, published in 2020. ISBN 978-1-898758-14-3.*

Reducing congestion is key to delivering reliable and predictable services and will need additional funding. Faster journeys are more productive for users and operators alike and can help to keep fares down as well as attracting extra users.

Recruitment and retention require investment in management, staff training and wage levels – keeping them attractive in local labour markets to offset the downsides of shift work and unsocial hours. There is also a need to develop skills and standards amongst local authorities and to ensure that their transport specialists are part of the authority's key decision-making processes.

Increasing Service Levels

Increasing service levels to meet accessibility needs and customer aspirations requires up-front funding, even if patronage growth could over time reduce the costs or even eventually make them self-funding. In Chapter 10, we have attempted to provide some estimates of what these costs might be, looking at four different scenarios in each of six separate market sectors.

The operating costs vary from a relatively modest £310m a year to extend the operating day by an average of one hour in areas outside London, through £1.6 billion a year to get the network back to pre-Covid levels, right up to £2.7 billion a year to restore all the cuts made since 2010. This option would also come with a capital expenditure requirement of between £3.0 and £3.8 billion to provide the necessary vehicles.

Decarbonising the Fleet

One of the biggest tasks the industry faces is decarbonisation. This means getting rid of older, more polluting vehicles and ultimately moving to zero-emissions sometime between 2035 and 2040.

In Chapter 11, we discuss how the industry's financial problems since Covid have added to an investment backlog that was already building, and our analysis showed a rising average fleet age. In 2023, this was in excess of eleven years in England outside London and in Wales, with London and Scotland showing over nine years. The result was a backlog of more than 10,000 more heavily polluting pre-Euro VI vehicles in service in March 2023.

Altogether, if a target of 100% zero emission buses by 2035 is to be reached, it creates a need for some 26,000 new zero-emission buses to be delivered by 2035, at a total cost we estimate to be around £13.7 billion - £9.8 billion in the markets outside London and another £3.8 billion for the capital. Operators and manufacturers are moving towards a more rapid deployment of zero-emission buses by repowering some of the existing fleet. Our analysis of the fleet using the criteria suggested for viable conversion shows that up to 5,700 vehicles might be suitable for this treatment which could save the industry some £1.4 billion in capital expenditure in the short term.

Delivering Modal Shift

The fourth task concerns modal shift as part of a move towards the targets set by the Climate Change Committee in the fifth and sixth carbon budgets. In Chapter 12, we offer a fresh and more nuanced analysis of what achievement of the targets might mean in terms for bus patronage, considering different journey lengths, durations and journey purposes. In summary, we suggest that:

- a 5% switch from current levels would result in growth of 668 million passengers from 2022/23 levels, taking the total to 4.41 billion, leaving the national total still well short of the pre-Covid total in 2018/19 of 4.79 billion
- under a 9% switch scenario, growth of 1.2 billion would take patronage to 4.95 billion, a total last seen as recently as 2017/18
- a 17% reduction in car use could really make a big difference, taking bus patronage to just over six billion, a figure last seen in the early 1980s.

The Threats

There are several threats to the future of the industry, most of which will be familiar to those who follow its fortunes.

- Continuing growth in car ownership, leading to increased traffic levels and congestion. As we note in Chapter 12, the DfT's 2022 set of National Road Traffic Projections[4], had a core scenario envisaging a 22% growth in traffic between 2025 and 2060, whilst congestion was predicted to increase by 27%
- Continuing resistance from the public towards measures which reallocate road space away from the private car or seek to impose additional charges on motorists
- The continuing pressure on local authority budgets which is likely to lead to further cuts in service levels as LTAs cut back on discretionary spending
- The future of local government finance in the light of concerns over the viability of Council Tax and the government's plans for more devolution, especially to Combined Authorities
- A growing disconnect between revenue and costs in the industry. Pressures on ministers and LTAs to keep fares "affordable" are in stark contrast to the recent surge in the costs of operation and the continued shortfall in passenger demand, creating a large funding gap. Setting fares in isolation from the costs of operation is a recipe for even greater dependence on government funding, with no certainty that this will be forthcoming.
- Short-term threats to ongoing funding of the industry, in the light of the current fiscal position and other high priority calls on the public purse. Specific uncertainties at the time of writing include:
  - The future of the £2 fare in England currently due to expire in December 2024
  - BSIP spending after March 2025 – either maintaining momentum in the 32 authorities that received first-round funding or enabling the remaining 46 to deliver on their ambitions
  - Whether there will be further rounds of government funding assistance for the introduction of Zero Emission Buses
  - The future of other funding, including Concessionary Fares and BSOG which were both already under review by the DfT before the 2024 General Election.

---

[4] See https://www.gov.uk/government/publications/national-road-traffic-projections

A Question of Money

In the end, it all comes down to money. It is idle to pretend that new legislation alone will deliver the required outcomes in the four areas we have discussed without funding to go with it.

Others suggest that franchising can be funded by central government and additional borrowing. It is argued that profits made from successful services could be used to cross-subsidise other less successful routes. However, since busy routes tend to be used by people on lower incomes, whilst less successful routes tend to run in more prosperous areas, this raises significant questions about social equity and income redistribution.

Franchise proposals published thus far favour the gross cost model and envisage the tendering authority owning both vehicles and depots – potentially creating a huge ongoing capital expenditure commitment alongside the commercial risks being shouldered.

In looking to the future, authorities should not overlook two important experiences:

- the London model, where the private sector has funded the huge investment made into the bus fleet, in partnership with TfL and its predecessors for the last 30 years
- the Jersey experience, in which the government moved away from the gross cost contract model to an innovative net cost model several years ago.

If the private sector is still deemed to have a role, then a policy platform needs to be developed that gives stability and certainty to incentivise investment, alongside a regulatory framework that permits investors to earn a return. Giving local transport authorities a permanent right to adopt a franchise model on a single committee or cabinet vote at any time would undermine this. There would be no stability to allow long-term investment decisions to be made, whilst there would be a risk that such uncertainty would drive the remaining SME operators – already nervous of the costs and risks of zero-emission vehicles - out of the industry.

Meanwhile, the new Chancellor of the Exchequer is seeking significant reductions in government spending and signalling significant increases in taxation. The Chancellor is actively seeking private sector investment in a revived private finance initiative approach to delivering investment in infrastructure.

Operators have made it clear repeatedly that they stand ready to work with authorities in whatever regulatory regime is in force to deliver the improvements. They just need a stable framework in which to do so.

Part A: Where We've Come From
1. The Market since 2010

1.1 Operator Income

Bus industry operating revenue comes in four broad categories:

- Income from passenger fares
- Central government grants (known as Bus Service Operators' Grant, or BSOG)
- Local government support for services, provided by county councils, unitary authorities, the Great London Authority and most mayoral combined authorities.
- Concessionary fares reimbursement, in which authorities pay the bus operators for income foregone when passholders travel for free.

During the period after 2010, income from all these sources fell – affecting every area of Great Britain and each of the four income categories. Thus, outside London, the numbers show that:

- Income from fares went down by 23.0% thanks to the combined effects of patronage oss and a reduction in yields.
- BSOG payments fell by 50.4%, thanks to the 20% cut in the rate paid and other reforms as well as the reductions in mileage operated
- Supported service expenditure fell by a 33.2%, as a result of spending cuts
- Income from concessionary fares reimbursement fell by 34.7% as a result of cuts in reimbursement rates and increases to the qualifying age in most of England, plus – since Covid – a significant loss of passengers

The details of the spending, and the cuts that have taken place, can be seen in both Figure A and Table 1 below.

The result of all this change for passengers has been a combination of fewer services and higher fares as local authorities slashed their supported service budgets and both they and operators attempted to recover the increased costs of operation from fewer passengers. It has proved to be a toxic combination, aided and abetted by increased traffic congestion and the widespread driver shortages that developed after the pandemic.

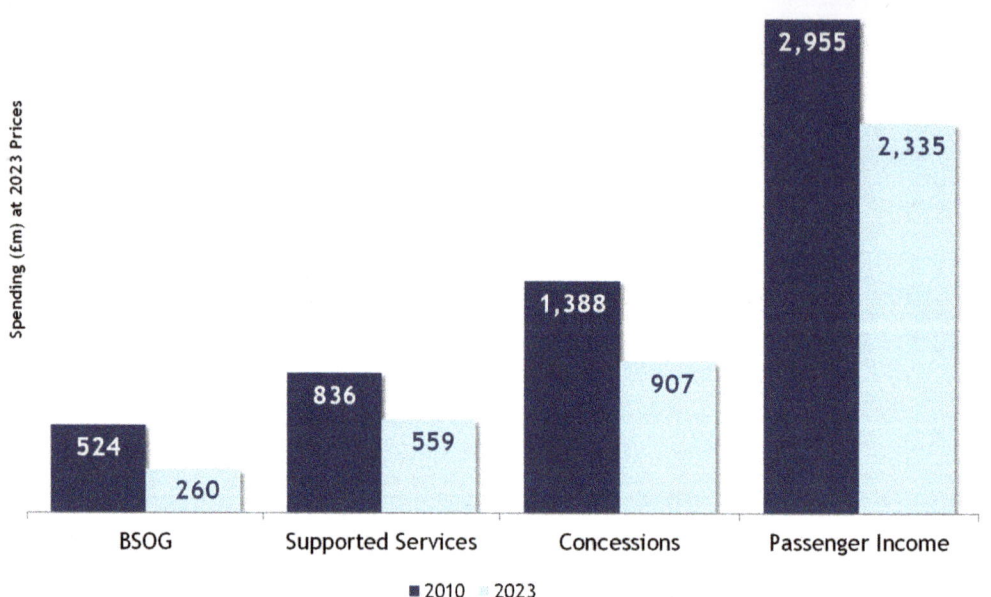

For sources, see table 1. In the graph, Covid recovery payments of £275m in 2023 are disregarded, as they ceased on 31 March 2023. £2 fare cap reimbursement included in Passenger Income for 2023 (£60m).

Table 1: Bus Industry Income
2009/10 v 2022/23 at Constant Prices (£m)

Item	London	English Mets	English Shires	Scotland	Wales	All Great Britain	GB Outside London
Year to 31 March 2010							
BSOG	149	147	277	75	25	673	524
Supported Services	923	183	533	83	36	1,760	836
Concessions	244	413	637	249	89	1,632	1,388
Sub-Total	**1,317**	**744**	**1,447**	**407**	**150**	**4,065**	**2,748**
Passenger Income	1,255	964	1,432	441	118	4,210	2,955
Total Income	**2,572**	**1,708**	**2,879**	**848**	**268**	**8,276**	**5,703**
Year to 31 March 2023							
BSOG	-	67	134	59	-	260	260
Supported Services	798	163	312	53	31	1,357	559
Concessions	140	265	317	265	60	1,047	907
Other †	-	83	130	92	30	335	335
Sub-total	**938**	**579**	**892**	**468**	**121**	**2,998**	**2,060**
Passenger Income ‡	1,212	671	1,249	280	74	3,487	2,275
Total Income	**2,150**	**1,250**	**2,141**	**748**	**196**	**6,485**	**4,335**
% changes							
BSOG	(100.0%)	(54.6%)	(51.8%)	(20.5%)	(100.0%)	(61.4%)	(50.4%)
Supported Services	(13.6%)	(10.9%)	(41.5%)	(36.3%)	(15.7%)	(22.9%)	(33.2%)
Concessions	(42.5%)	(35.8%)	(50.3%)	6.0%	(31.9%)	(35.9%)	(34.7%)
Sub-Total	**(28.8%)**	**(22.2%)**	**(38.4%)**	**15.0%**	**(19.0%)**	**(26.2%)**	**(25.0%)**
Passenger Income	(3.4%)	(30.4%)	(12.8%)	(36.5%)	(37.3%)	(17.2%)	(23.0%)
Total Income	**(16.4%)**	**(26.8%)**	**(25.6%)**	**(11.7%)**	**(27.1%)**	**(21.6%)**	**(24.0%)**

Source: Passenger Transport Monitor analysis of figures from Department for Transport Annual Bus Statistics, Sheets BUS04 and BUS05, Scottish Transport Statistics, Welsh Transport Statistics. Welsh Covid payment from Welsh Government budget reports.

Figures are in constant prices at June 2023 levels, adjusted by use of the GDP Deflator.

† - Residual Covid recovery payments. All ceased on 31 March 2023. In England, payments published by DfT at national level only. Estimated split for Covid payments between PTE (38.3%) and Shire areas (61.7%) based on 2018/19 passenger revenue.

‡ - For England outside London, also includes £60m worth of reimbursement for the £2 fare cap (Jan-Mar 2023 only). Fare cap payment apportioned between PTE (41.4%) and Shire areas (58.6%) based on paying passenger numbers in 2022/23.

1.2 Changes in Service Levels

1.2.1 Overview

The fall in service levels has been much discussed and is plain for all to see in the numbers for kilometres run on local bus services. Across GB outside London, there was a reduction of 27.7% in kilometres run between 2009/10 and 2022/23. The cuts in the supported networks were even greater, at 49.8%, and this figure rose to over 60% in some areas of the English Shires. The details are in Table 2 below.

Table 2: Bus Kilometres Run
Millions, 2009/10 v 2022/23

Item	London	English Mets	English Shires	Scotland	Wales	All Great Britain	GB Outside London
Year to 31 March 2010							
Commercial	0	475	768	302	81	1,627	1,627
Supported	479	94	303	74	43	993	515
Total	**479**	**569**	**1,071**	**377**	**124**	**2,620**	**2,141**
Year to 31 March 2023							
Commercial	0	335	664	231	61	1,290	1,290
Supported	454	62	129	44	23	713	258
Total	**454**	**397**	**793**	**275**	**84**	**2,003**	**1,549**
% changes							
Commercial	-	(29.5%)	(13.6%)	(23.7%)	(24.9%)	(20.7%)	(20.7%)
Supported	(5.1%)	(34.3%)	(57.4%)	(40.8%)	(45.9%)	(28.3%)	(49.8%)
Total	**(5.1%)**	**(30.3%)**	**(25.9%)**	**(27.1%)**	**(32.2%)**	**(23.5%)**	**(27.7%)**

Source: Department for Transport, Annual Bus Statistics, Sheet BUS02

1.2.2 The Urban/Rural Split

The urban/rural split figures are provided by the DfT using the ONS Rural-Urban Classification system. Further details of how this works can be found in Appendix D.

The analysis is shown in Table 3 below and shows that rural areas have suffered harsh cuts in supported service networks since 2010, losing more than 56% of their tendered networks, compared with 34% in the PTE areas, but over 63% in areas covered by other urban authorities.

1.2.3 The Commercial/Supported Split

There's a big difference when it comes to commercially operated mileage, though. Here, the reductions in commercial services in rural areas have been much lower, at between 10% and 13% compared with 16% in other urban areas and 29% in PTE areas. As a consequence, more than 80% of the remaining rural bus services are commercially operated, as compared with between 67% and 70% in 2010.

Table 3: Urban/Rural Split in Kilometres Run
England, Millions, 2009/10 v 2022/23

Item	Met Areas	Other Mainly Urban	Urban with Significant Rural	Largely or Mainly Rural	England Outside London
Year to 31 March 2010					
Commercial	475	316	241	212	1,243
Supported	94	96	102	104	397
Total	**569**	**412**	**343**	**316**	**1,640**
Year to 31 March 2023					
Commercial	335	265	216	183	999
Supported	62	35	48	46	191
Total	**397**	**300**	**264**	**229**	**1,190**
% changes					
Commercial	(29.5%)	(16.0%)	(10.4%)	(13.5%)	(19.6%)
Supported	(34.3%)	(63.5%)	(52.7%)	(56.3%)	(51.9%)
Total	**(30.3%)**	**(27.1%)**	**(23.0%)**	**(27.6%)**	**(27.5%)**

Source: Department for Transport Annual Bus Statistics, Sheet BUS02km. Definition of urban/rural split based on the 2011 Rural-Urban Classification for Local Authority Districts in England, published by the ONS.

Table 4: Commercial/Supported Proportions of Bus Kilometres
England by Urban/Rural Split, 2009/10 v 2022/23

Item	Met Areas	Other Mainly Urban	Urban with significant rural	Largely or Mainly Rural	England Outside London
Year to 31 March 2010					
Commercial	83.5%	76.6%	70.1%	67.0%	71.7%
Supported	16.5%	23.4%	29.9%	33.0%	28.3%
Total	**100.0%**	**100.0%**	**100.0%**	**100.0%**	**100.0%**
Year to 31 March 2023					
Commercial	84.4%	88.3%	81.7%	80.1%	83.7%
Supported	15.6%	11.7%	18.3%	19.9%	16.3%
Total	**100.0%**	**100.0%**	**100.0%**	**100.0%**	**100.0%**

Source: Figures derived from Table 3 above

1.3 Changes in Passenger Numbers

1.3.1 The Overall Picture

The decline in patronage, both before and since the pandemic, is often discussed, and it has indeed been substantial – totalling almost a third across Great Britain outside London, whilst the capital itself has lost a fifth of its 2010 patronage.

It is also instructive to look at the components of the total number, in particular, travel on concessionary passes, youth and other concession schemes and the fare-paying remainder.

The numbers are shown in Table 5 below. Wales saw the biggest drop, with a 47.8% fall, followed by the English Met areas on 34.7% and Scotland on 34.3%.

In London, the fall was smaller, at 21.1%. However, patronage in the capital was still growing in 2010, and did not peak until 2013/14, when the total reached 2,384 million. The fall since that peak is 25.9%.

1.3.2 Elderly and Disabled Travellers

The biggest patronage losses have occurred amongst elderly and disabled travellers, especially in the Met Areas and Wales, where numbers more than halved between 2009/10 and 2022/23. They all but halved in the English Shires as well but were only 14% down in London. Again, though, journey volumes in London had carried on growing throughout the decade, peaking at 360m journeys immediately before the pandemic. The fall since then has been 24.0%.

One factor driving the reduction was a progressive increase in the age at which people became eligible for a pass. In England (except West Midlands and Merseyside), these changes between 2010 and 2019 reduced the population entitled to a pass by 21.2%, or 2.4m people.

1.3.3 Youth Schemes

Patronage on youth schemes shows significant growth, largely as a result of the introduction of the under 22s concession in Scotland, where there had been no concession previously. This started in January 2022. Where schemes were established in 2010, patronage has gone down – by 14.4% in the PTE Areas and most notably by 23.8% in London. As with the adult fare payers, though, numbers in London carried on growing after 2009/10, peaking at 446 million in 2013/14: the fall since then stands at 31.3%.

1.3.4 Fare-Paying Passengers

Turning finally to fare-paying passengers, the apparent large loss in Scotland is at least partially the result of the introduction of the Under 22s free scheme in 2022. Aside from that, Wales once again showed the largest reduction, at 47.7%, followed by the English Met areas on 30.7%. The smallest loss occurred in the English Shires, on 20.6%. The London figure shows a loss of 21.9%, but the loss from the 2013/14 peak is 26.0%.

1.3.5 The Urban/Rural Split

Looking at the urban/rural split for England outside London, we see that the biggest losses occurred in the areas designated "urban with significant rural", where patronage fell by almost 37% between 2009/10 and 2022/23. These areas, coloured grey on the ONS map at Appendix D, Figure A, cover a large part of the South East on the periphery of Greater London together with similar areas near other major conurbations. As we have already seen, the conurbations lost 34.7%. Perhaps surprisingly in the light of the mileage reductions discussed above, the loss of passengers in the largely or mainly rural areas was restricted to 28.8%, whilst the urban areas outside the Mets saw the smallest losses, on 25.7%.

Table 5: Bus Patronage by Type of Passenger
Millions, 2009/10 v 2022/23

Year to 31 March	London	English Mets	English Shires	Scotland	Wales	GB outside London
Total Passengers (millions)						
2010	2,238.2	1,062.1	1,313.3	458.0	116.9	2,950.3
2023	1,766.1	693.7	923.4	300.7	61.0	1,978.9
% change	(21.1%)	(34.7%)	(29.7%)	(34.3%)	(47.8%)	(32.9%)
Elderly & Disabled Passengers (millions)						
2010	318.0	291.7	440.8	153.3	48.7	1,249.3
2023	273.6	145.7	224.1	96.9	23.3	763.6
% change	(14.0%)	(50.0%)	(49.2%)	(36.8%)	(52.1%)	(38.9%)
Youth and Other Concessions (millions)						
2010	402.4	87.4	27.9	0.4	1.8	519.6
2023	306.6	74.8	28.5	49.3	3.0	462.3
% change	(23.8%)	(14.4%)	2.1%	100.0%	64.8%	(11.0%)
Fare-Paying Passengers (millions)						
2010	1,517.8	683.0	844.5	304.4	66.3	1,181.4
2023	1,185.9	473.1	670.8	154.5	34.7	753.0
% change	(21.9%)	(30.7%)	(20.6%)	(49.2%)	(47.7%)	(36.3%)

Source: DfT Annual Bus Statistics, Sheet BUS01

Table 6: Bus Patronage by Urban/Rural Split
England, 2009/10 v 2022/23

Year to 31 March	Met Areas	Other Mainly Urban	Urban with Significant Rural	Largely or Mainly Rural	England Outside London
Millions of Passenger Journeys					
2010	1,062	631	395	287	2,375
2023	694	469	250	204	1,617
% change	(34.7%)	(25.7%)	(36.8%)	(28.8%)	(31.9%)
% Breakdown of Patronage by Sector					
2010	44.7%	26.6%	16.6%	12.1%	100.0%
2023	42.9%	29.0%	15.4%	12.6%	100.0%

Source: Department for Transport Annual Bus Statistics, Sheet BUS01. Definition of urban/rural split based on the 2011 Rural-Urban Classification for Local Authority Districts in England, published by the ONS. See Appendix for more details.

1.4 Fares: The DfT Fares Indices

For many years, the DfT has collected data on changes in fare levels from bus operators and published the results as part of the annual bus statistics – with quarterly updates. For the whole of the period from 2010 until the onset of Covid, bus fares across all areas increased ahead of inflation. At their peak, the fares indices showed real-term increases of over 22% in the English Shires, 16% in the Met Areas, 14% in Scotland and 10% in Wales. The exception was London, where the change of Mayor in 2016 brought in Sadiq Khan's five-year fares freeze, followed by one increase in 2020/21.

Then came Covid, emergency funding and greater intervention by government and local authorities – including the introduction of free travel for the under 22s in Scotland from January 2022, other youth discount schemes and the £2 fares cap in England from January 2023, currently running until December 2024. The graph at Figure B below shows the movement in real-term fares indices over the period since 2010 in each market sector – from which it can be seen that, by March 2023, the fare indices were below 2010 levels in real terms.

It will be appreciated that the indices are calculated on a basket of fares and will not necessarily reflect what has happened to the fares charged for specific journeys.

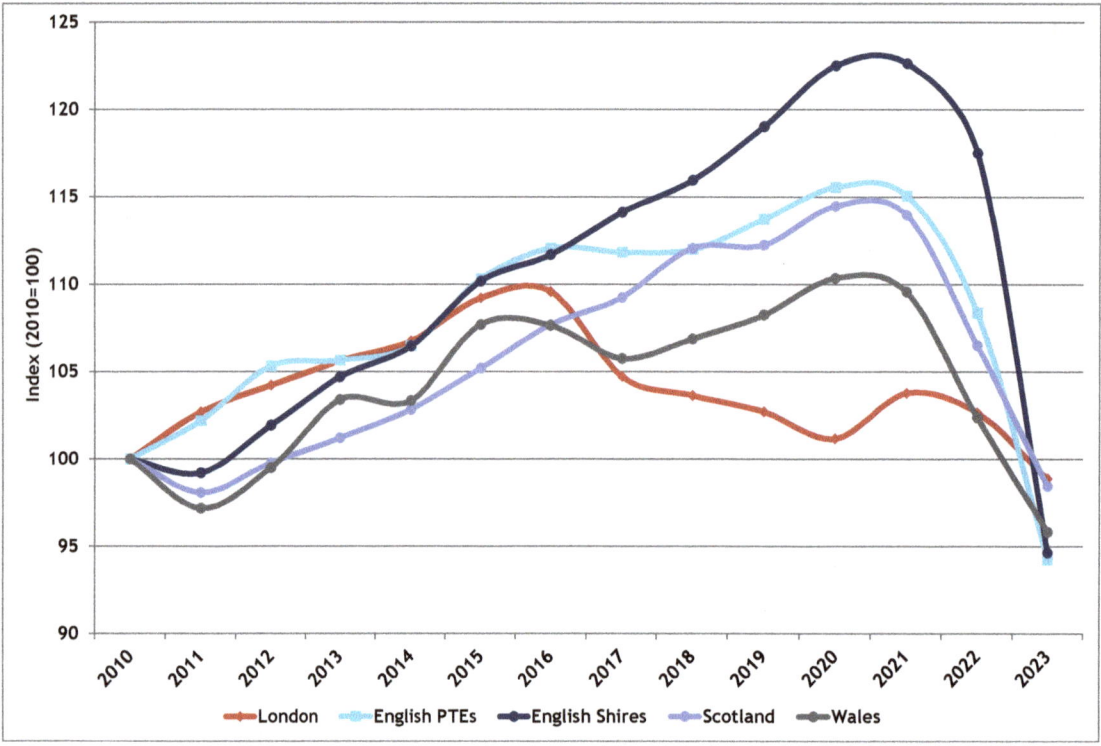

Figure B: Real-Term Changes in Bus Fare Levels since 2009/10
Financial Years. Index, 2010=100. Movement in Constant Prices.

Source: Department for Transport Annual Bus Statistics, Table BUS04dii, rebased by PTIS to 2010.

An examination of more recent quarterly trends in fare levels is provided in the charts at Figure C (for the three English sectors) and Figure D (for Scotland, Wales and GB as a whole) below. The indices have been rebased to March 2019 = 100.

On the English chart, the effect of the introduction of the £2 fare cap in the January to March quarter of 2023 is particularly clear especially in the English Shires. In the PTE areas, the fall was less precipitate, and it was preceded and accompanied by other locally funded measures as part of the partnerships developed as part of the post-Covid recovery plans and the early effects of the BSIP process.

In Scotland, the effect of the introduction of the free under 22s concession is clear in January 2022, mirrored by the effects of an overall fares standstill in Wales as part of their post-Covid plans. However, in Scotland, the effects on fares of the ending of post-Covid funding in March 2023 are clearly visible. Fares charged to the remaining paying passengers were driven higher between March and June 2023.

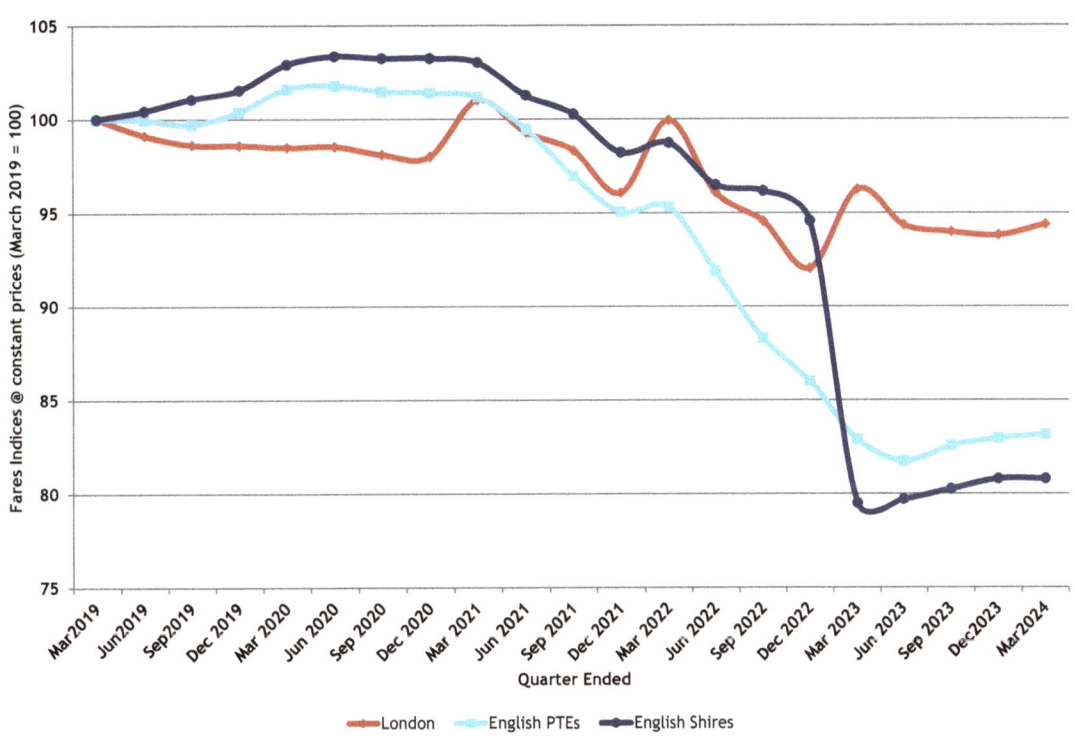

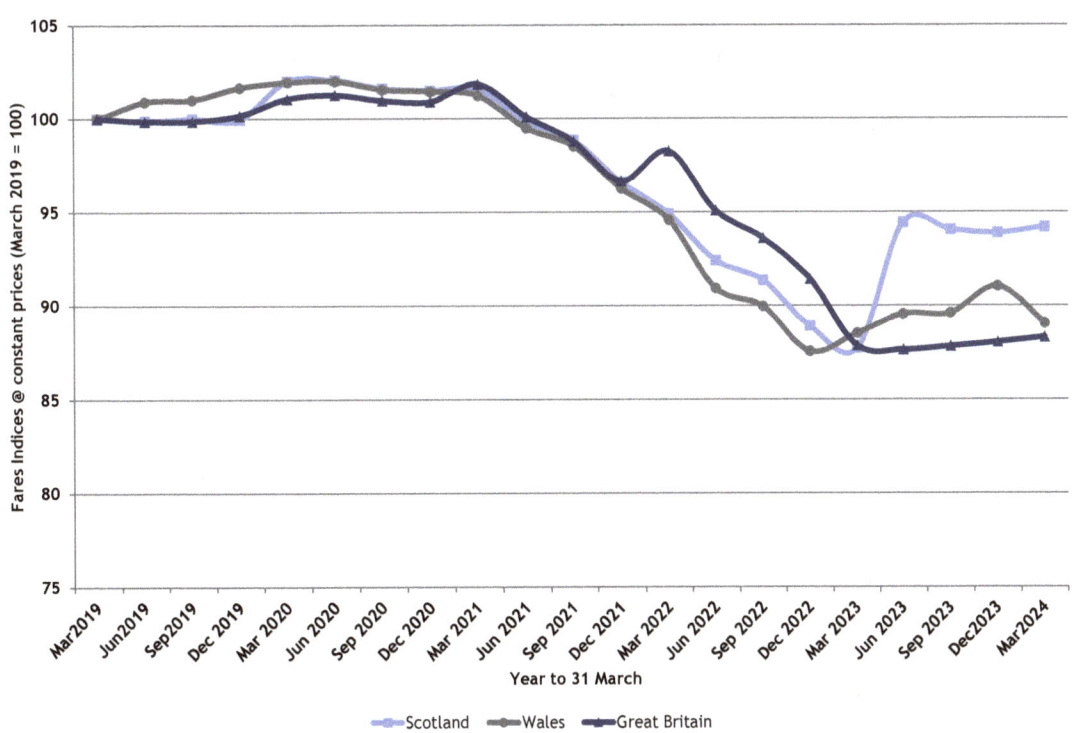

1.5 Revenue Yields

The fares indices can only give a partial view of bus fares, allowing us to track changes in the levels of fares charged. However, customers can and do choose different types of ticket which may save them money, whilst journey patterns shift and change – particularly in the aftermath of the pandemic. This can be measured by the revenue which the fares yield, which can be measured in two ways: average revenue per passenger journey, or average revenue per passenger kilometre. The latter measure might be considered to be the better means of tracking changes, since it takes into account shifts in average journey lengths (though these are remarkably stable over time), payment methods and ticket types.

The figures for these are contained in Table 7 below. The income total is calculated as the sum of passenger revenue and concessionary reimbursement from the operating revenue discussed in Table 1 above, which is then divided by the number of passenger journeys, or the number of passenger kilometres recorded in the annual bus statistics.

As can be seen, whilst all areas have seen a real term fall in passenger income, the outturns in terms of yields are markedly different. London saw the smallest fall in passenger income, thanks in part to stability in its concessionary fares scheme, whilst managing to increase yields on both measures. In the rest of England, income per passenger journey increased, but the per passenger km measure was remarkably stable. More substantial increases in yields were achieved in Scotland and Wales by both measures.

The trends over the years after 2009/10 are illustrated in the chart at Figure E below.

Table 7: Passenger Revenue Yields, 2009/10 v 2022/23
Constant (June 2023) Prices

Year to 31 March	London	English Mets	English Shires	Scotland	Wales	GB Outside London
Passenger income £m (fares and concessionary reimbursement)						
2010	1,499	1,377	2,069	690	207	4,344
2023	1,352	937	1,566	545	135	3,181
% change	(9.8%)	(32.0%)	(24.3%)	(21.1%)	(35.0%)	(26.8%)
Passenger income per passenger journey (£)						
2010	0.670	1.297	1.575	1.507	1.774	1.472
2023	0.766	1.350	1.695	1.811	2.207	1.608
% change	14.3%	4.1%	7.6%	20.2%	24.4%	9.2%
Passenger income per Passenger Kilometre (£)						
2010	0.157	0.221	0.204	0.194	0.225	0.208
2023	0.178	0.226	0.200	0.259	0.276	0.218
% change	13.4%	2.1%	(2.0%)	33.6%	23.1%	4.9%

Source: PTIS analysis of Annual Bus Statistics, DfT, Sheets BUS05 and BUS01 and Scottish and Welsh Transport Statistics.

Figure E: Revenue Yields per Passenger Kilometre by Sector
2009/10 to 2022/23, Constant (June 2023) Prices

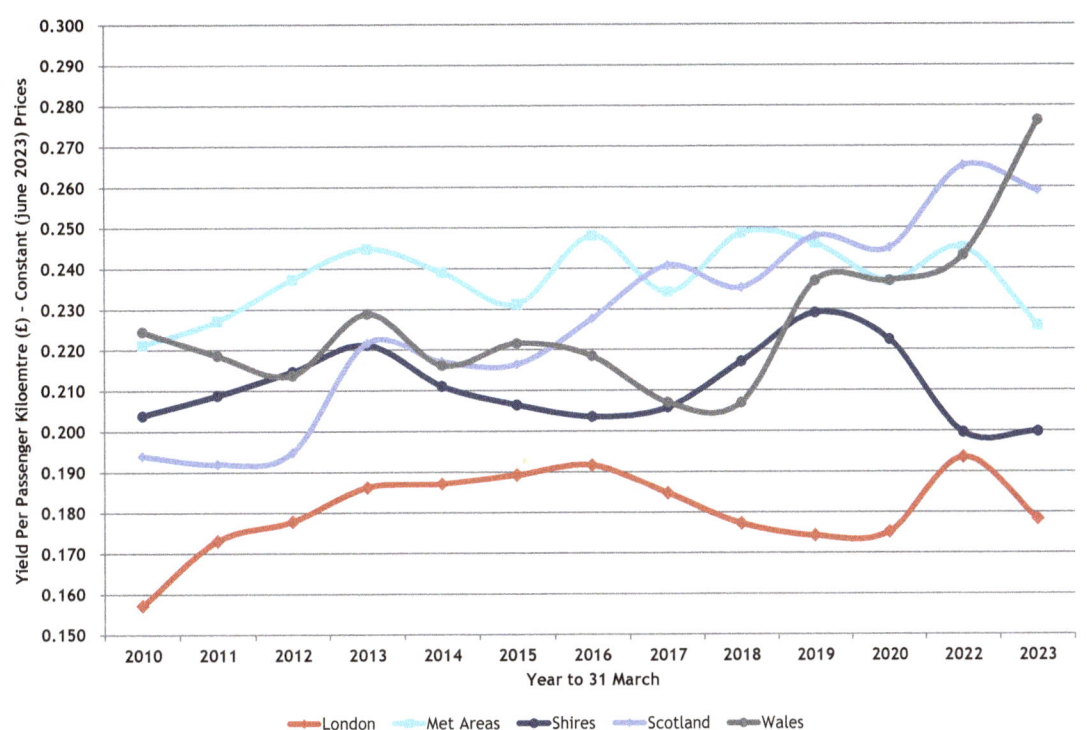

Source: PTIS analysis of Annual Bus Statistics, DfT, Sheets BUS05 and BUS01 and Scottish and Welsh Transport Statistics. Year ended 31 March 2021 omitted as Covid and lockdowns distorted the figures.

This page intentionally blank

2. Bus Operating Costs

2.1 The Overall Picture

Changes in cost levels have two elements – changes caused by the *unit costs* of operation and changes in the *scale* of the operation (kilometres run, vehicles owned, etc). Figures for total costs of operation are a function of both these factors – and we know, of course, that the volume of services provided has fallen quite sharply since 2009/10. DfT's published statistics enable us to measure unit costs in two ways – per kilometre operated and per passenger journey. The details of all three elements are contained in Table 8 below.

Table 8: Bus Operating Costs by Sector
2009/10 to 2022/23, Constant (June 2023) Prices

Year to 31 March	London	English Mets	English Shires	Scotland	Wales	GB Outside London
Total Operating Costs (£m)						
2010	2,496	1,556	2,279	751	193	4,779
2023	2,208	1,231	2,111	674	153	4,168
% change	(11.5%)	(20.9%)	(7.4%)	(10.3%)	(20.8%)	(12.8%)
Unit Operating Costs, per kilometre (£)						
2010	5.213	2.735	2.127	1.822	0.563	2.255
2023	4.861	3.102	2.661	2.243	0.580	2.535
% change	(6.7%)	13.4%	25.1%	23.1%	2.9%	12.4%
Unit Operating Costs, per passenger journey (£)						
2010	1.115	1.465	1.735	1.639	1.654	1.620
2023	1.250	1.774	2.286	2.241	2.508	2.107
% change	12.1%	21.1%	31.7%	36.7%	51.6%	30.0%

Sources: Department for Transport Annual Bus Statistics, Sheet BUS04. London figures from annual accounts of LBSL.

As can be seen, the reductions in service provision discussed in Table 2 above are reflected in the real-term reductions in expenditure in the first section of Table 8 above, covering total operating costs: in two sectors – Wales and the English Met areas – the fall is over 20%.

However, it is a very different story when we look at the unit operating costs. In the first measure, costs per kilometre run, with increases of over 20% in the English Shires and Scotland, 13.4% in the Met areas and 2.9% in Wales. Only in London do these figures show a saving, of 6.7%.

The figures for cost per passenger journey show even larger increases. It is this figure which explains why increases in fares have been necessary over these years. Unit costs have risen whilst the number of passengers has fallen, meaning that the industry has needed to recover its costs from ever fewer passengers.

2.2 The Structure of Bus Industry Costs

Data from the Confederation of Passenger Transport's twice-yearly Cost Monitor survey enables us to gain an up to date picture of the structure of industry costs. Their graph showing the structure is reproduced as Figure F below.

It will be seen that labour costs dominate the total, accounting for 54.1% of total costs. Direct running costs such as fuel oil and spare parts account for a further 17.8%, with fixed and semi-variable items responsible for the balance of 28.1%.

Figure F: Bus Industry Cost Structure, February 2024, GB Outside London

Source: Bus Industry Costs in February 2024, *CPT and 2FM Limited, July 2024.* https://www.cpt-uk.org/

2.3 The Importance of Labour Costs

The predominance of labour costs is inevitable, given the industry's reliance on its people to deliver services, maintain the vehicles and manage and administer service delivery – including ensuring compliance with the significant and growing regulatory burdens placed on operators.

Historically, wages and salaries have risen more quickly than prices, with the result that bus industry operating costs have risen by more than general inflation. Over the years, this has caused financial difficulties, especially in the public sector, when attempts have been made to tie public spending to inflation targets. Measures of inflation such as CPI are wholly inadequate to measure changes in bus industry costs.

Both operators and the public have had a brutal reminder over the last three years of the consequences of an inability to recruit sufficient drivers – unreliable services, short-notice cancellations, low morale and poor customer relations. It is a toxic combination – and one which the industry has experienced all too often over the years, especially at times of full employment.

The crisis in driver recruitment that followed the end of the pandemic in 2021 was driven by a number of factors, including:

- delays in the documentation for and testing of new recruits at DVLA

- competition for trained and skilled drivers from the HGV market, including offers of wage rates which bus operators could not match
- reduced immigration from Europe following the UK's decision to leave the EU
- a loss of staff who failed to return after furlough
- the number of retirements as a result of an ageing workforce
- inability of operators to match market rates for labour in the face of collapsed revenue and funding uncertainty
- reduced labour supply as long term sickness and growth of economic inactivity took their toll.

The position has eased since the worst days of driver shortages, but the problem is still there to some extent, and probably always will be – especially at times of full employment. Aside from the level of wages, working conditions – such as early and late shifts, weekend working and the stress of dealing with timekeeping and heavy traffic.

2.4 The Importance of Time and Speed

Historically, bus industry costs were benchmarked and measured as a charge per mile. Changes in average cost per mile were regularly reported, and these numbers were used as the basis for calculating fares and fare increases throughout the 1950s and 1960s.

In the early 1970s, as cost accountancy became a more exact science, it became clear that time rather than distance was the major driver of bus operating costs. This was because labour was the industry's largest cost item, and the size of the wage bill was driven by the number of hours worked – a much more important figure than the number of miles run.

Such an approach was particularly useful when it came to splitting costs over different routes, networks or depots.

The number of hours for which operators need to run their buses is mainly a function of speed. This will determine:

- how long the bus will take to run from one terminus to another
- how many revenue-earning trips can be run by each bus in a day
- how many drivers will be required to provide the service.

The average speed at which buses can run will depend on a combination of factors, including:

- the types of road on which it runs (including local topography)
- how congested the roads are
- what parking restrictions there are and how these are enforced
- the number of stops
- how long the bus must wait at each stop.

A worked example of the effect that changes in speed and journey time can have on operating costs is provided in Appendix B. This shows that where it is necessary to put one extra bus into operating a service, operating costs increase by 21%. Adding another one as speeds slowed further resulted in another increase, so that they are 42% higher than the base case.

We can see from our worked example in Appendix B what a crucial difference the speed of operation makes to our ability to run successful, viable bus services. As traffic congestion increases, speeds deteriorate and punctuality declines. As a result, more resources are required to maintain service levels, and more revenue is therefore needed to cover the costs of operation – which means that more passengers are needed to maintain viability. The big problem, however, is that as speeds fall and journey times get longer, buses are less attractive to people, and therefore passenger numbers are liable to fall rather than increase.

When this happens, the only way that the bus company can earn the revenue it needs is to put prices up. Even though revenue increases, the number of passengers falls again, so reinforcing a cycle of decline. This is illustrated in Figure G below.

By the same token, of course, the introduction of bus priorities and other measures that enable buses to go faster can deliver significant cost savings, as well as making the service more attractive to the public.

Figure G: The Bus Industry's Vicious Circle

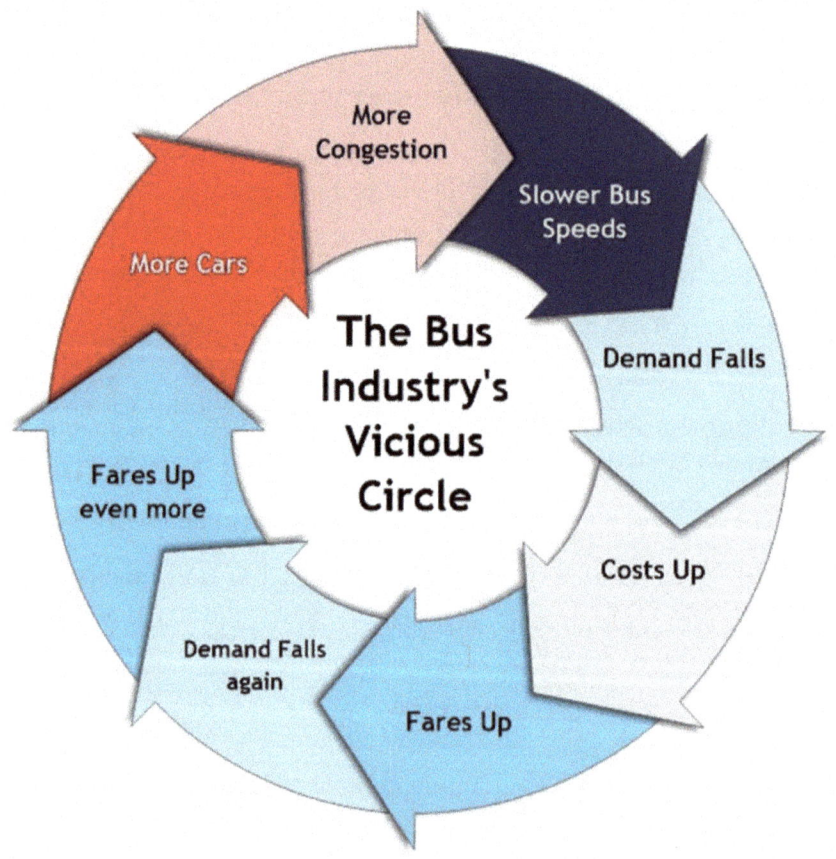

3. The Need for Profit

3.1 Why is profit necessary?

To provide a bus service, any operator needs a set of resources:

- Buses to run the service
- Depot in which to park and maintain the buses
- Other equipment such as a ticket machine

The operator needs money to fund these, also known as capital. Capital is borrowed from shareholders (which may be the local authority, the government or private enterprise) and lenders. As well as eventually repaying the loans, the act of borrowing creates obligations to:

- Pay interest on loans
- Reward shareholders (dividends)

Taken together, these two comprise the cost of capital.

At some point, the buses will wear out and require replacement. The depot will have to be maintained. A prudent business makes provision for such future expenditure by putting some spare money by every year so that when the time comes some funds will be available.

Thus, bus companies need to earn more money in revenue than they spend in costs, so as to:

- provide funds for the replacement and renewal of the equipment needed to carry on and expand the business
- pay interest on its borrowings
- repay the loans it has taken out
- provide for reserves to enable the company to survive in the bad times
- reward the shareholders of the business for their investment and risk.

3.1.2 The Investment Agenda

There has been, and remains, a clear need to invest in the re-equipment of the industry. This section looks at what has been achieved and what will be required in the short and medium term.

Though fleet age has traditionally been viewed as the indicator of the need for replacement of vehicles, this was largely based on the days of composite or wooden construction in bus bodywork, which effectively limited the period for cost-effective retention of vehicles to between 12 and 15 years.

All-metal construction, modern methods of corrosion protection and the use of aluminium (pioneered 70 years ago in the original London Routemaster bus) means that vehicle lives can be much longer.

Decisions concerning replacement therefore require other justification, which are primarily derived from a business case analysis, so that the investment can deliver a return.

Key factors in such decisions are:

- Contractual – required as part of Enhanced Partnership (EP) agreements or by tendering authorities such as Transport for London or Transport for Greater Manchester

- Financial – savings in maintenance costs such as replacement of components, cost and availability of spare parts

- Commercial – revenue (for example, operators reported revenue gains from the introduction of low-floor buses) and market potential (for example, front line intensive service, low rural or schools use)

- Regulatory – because older vehicles do not meet current accessibility or emissions standards. This is particularly relevant in the light of moves towards Net Zero, requiring investment in zero emission vehicles. Regulations constantly change – witness the recent addition of Accessible Passenger Information Regulations. A previous example was the deadline for the removal of step access buses. This was set to meet the requirements of the Disability Discrimination Act. This came into force in 2015 for single deck buses and at the end of 2016 for double deckers. The requirement for coaches deployed on scheduled services came into force in 2020.

Thus, though age is no longer a determinant of replacement decisions, it remains nevertheless a useful indicator of both the current state of the fleet and likely future investment requirements. The figures for the total fleet size and average age in 2009/10 and 2022/23 are compared in Table 9 below. It will be seen that the average age of the fleet across Great Britain outside London rose from 8.2 years in 2009/10 to 11.3 in 2022/23. In London, the age has moved from 6.1 to 9.2, whilst Scotland has seen a rise from 7.8 to 9.0 years. This was against a target of eight years

Table 9: Fleet Size and Average Age, 2009/10 v 2022/23

	London	English Mets	English Shires	Scotland	Wales	GB Outside London
Year to 31 March 2010						
Fleet Size (000s)	9.6	10.3	19.4	5.6	2.2	37.4
Average Age	6.1	7.7	8.4	7.8	9.0	8.2
Year to 31 March 2023						
Fleet Size (000s)	8.8	7.7	13.6	3.2	1.5	26.0
Average Age	9.2	11.4	11.8	9.0	11.1	11.3
% Changes						
Fleet Size	-8%	-25%	-30%	-43%	-32%	-30%
Average Age	51%	48%	40%	15%	23%	38%

Source: PTIS analysis of Department for Transport Annual Bus Statistics 2023, Sheet BUS06. 2009/10 figures from 2010 edition, Sheets BUS0602 and BUS0605.

Lower levels of investment in new vehicles are clearly responsible for the ageing fleet, and there may be a number of reasons for this:

- Lower profit levels throughout the years after 2010, reducing available funds and borrowing capacity, made worse by the Covid pandemic and revised perceptions of risk
- Delays to decision-making, ordering and during and after the lockdowns.
- Increased unit costs (especially for zero emission buses) meaning that fewer vehicles can be bought for a given level of funding
- Retrofitting of earlier vehicles to meet Euro VI diesel emission standards, enabling life extension of older vehicles.

Looking ahead, the move towards electric vehicles, whether powered by batteries or fuel cells, is now irreversible, and forms a central plank of the government's decarbonisation plans. This is discussed further in Chapter 11 below.

3.1.3 Interest Charges

The payment of interest on borrowings has a direct relationship with investment levels.

Few, if any, companies have access to sufficient cash to buy the equipment themselves, so they must borrow - either in the form of loans or finance leases or hire purchase deals.

These debts attract interest charges - and lenders will take a critical look at the level of profits available to cover these charges before being prepared to make the loan. This is the business equivalent of a bank or a building society looking at an individual's income levels before granting them a mortgage.

Recent events in the financial markets have meant that – again like mortgages – lenders are taking a much tougher look at borrowers' ability to pay their interest charges from profits and tightening their criteria. This is a situation which of course makes life considerably more difficult, especially when profit levels are already falling because of a reduction in demand for travel.

In addition, the loans must be repaid (typically, in the case of a new bus, over five years), and the cash to make the repayments must be generated from the difference between the company's income and expenditure.

3.1.4 Transfers to Reserves

It is the fate of all transport operators to see patronage and revenue fluctuate in line with the fluctuations of the wider economy.

Demand for transport is, after all, derived from the public's wish to do other things, such as go to work, school or college, go shopping or just have a good time. And the stark fact is that if the public does these things less often, they will travel less often and both the demand for services and the revenue they earn will fall.

Therefore, like most sensible people in their home lives, any prudent business will make provision in 'good years' for 'lean' ones which might lie ahead.

3.1.5 Rewards for Shareholders

Lastly, the shareholders of the business need to be rewarded. At its most basic, the level of this reward needs to be higher than shareholders could earn by leaving their money into the bank or building society – both to persuade people to invest in the business, and to reflect the additional risks attached to investing in a business as opposed to just a savings account.

In practice, other factors will be involved, including the rewards that shareholders could earn from investing in other companies or other industries. Contrary to many preconceptions about shareholders, the vast majority of shares these days are held by organisations such as employee share ownership schemes, pension funds, unit trusts and investment trusts who are investing in shares on behalf of millions of ordinary people throughout the world.

3.2 Sustainable Profits

There has been little consensus since 1986 as to what the appropriate level of profit in the bus industry should be, which has caused some problems in stakeholder relationships over the years.

In fact, it is perfectly possible to work out the levels of profit a bus company needs to make. In other industries the economic regulators have been making such calculations for some 30 years, since the first privatisation of utility companies created the need for such regulators in the mid-1980s.

Over the years since 2010, therefore, *Passenger Transport Monitor* has tried to show how a target return on capital employed can be calculated, and then how this translates into a target operating profit margin – which is the most widely understood and easy to calculate measurement of performance. An important element is also to explain the effect of different methods of funding assets on the profit levels needed.

The analysis has been reviewed and updated once more in the light of current economic situation and the changes in cost levels and interest rates over the last five years. The results of this exercise are explained in detail in Appendix A.

The analysis uses what we call the ARCC Approach, which is a methodology built round four questions:

- **ASSETS**: What assets does the company need to provide its service?
- **RETURN**: What level of return is required on those assets to cover the cost of capital?
- **COST**: How much does the business cost to run?
- **CAPITAL**: What funds will the company need to borrow and on what terms?

Armed with those four pieces of data, it is then possible to determine:

- what the profits should be
- how much revenue the company needs in order to meet these obligations and targets, given its level of operating costs.

The methodology is illustrated in graphic form at Figure H below.

It is important to note that this analysis and approach holds good ***whatever the regulatory regime in force***. Thus, the decisions on service levels and network design that determine the *Asset Base Required* can be made by a commercial operator or by a tendering authority such as Transport for London. The *Revenue Required* can come in the form of individual fares paid by passengers, concessionary fares reimbursement and other grants, or as "cost plus" payments by tendering authorities, as in London.

Figure H: The Need for Profits in the Bus Industry - the ARCC Analysis

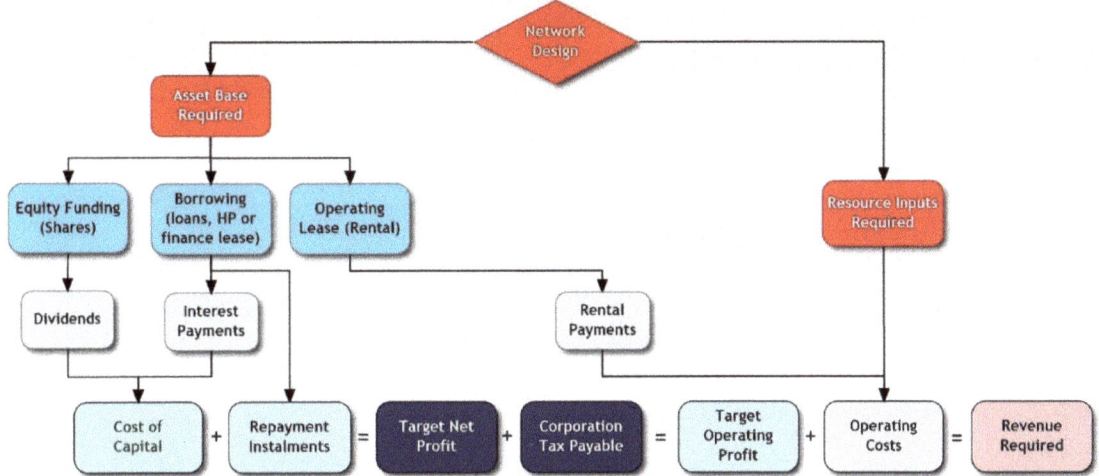

3.3 Profits under a Franchised Regime

It has argued by many over the years that operating buses under a franchised regime would be cheaper than the commercial/tendered combination that has been used since 1986. The fundamental principles of the model are set out in Figure H above. However, there would be two areas in which the model might vary: asset ownership and borrowing costs.

3.3.1 Asset Ownership

Under a franchised regime, there are basically two models:

- The tendering authority owns the assets (vehicles, depots etc) and rents then to the contracted operator (as in Greater Manchester)

- The operator owns the assets and uses them to supply the services to the tendering authority as specified in the contract (as used in London).

Having assets owned by the tendering authority reduces the capital employed by the operator and therefore reduces the profit they need to earn. However, the asset still has to be financed and accounted for by the tendering authority. There are two other arguments deployed in favour of authority ownership:

- Public sector bodies can always borrow more cheaply than private sector entities

- The lack of large upfront financing requirements enables a wider range of operators to compete for available contracts, so encouraging competition.

However, where public sector borrowing is subject to limits imposed by the Treasury on wider macro-economic grounds (as has happened frequently in the past), this can prevent the implementation of asset replacement and maintenance plans, resulting in poorer service quality and higher day to day operating costs.

3.4 Use of Operating Leases

At the same time, the asset(s) can be held under an operating lease from a third party finance house ("the lessor"). This means that:

- The lessor owns the property, and the lessee uses it for a fixed time.

- The lessee records rental payments as expenses.

- The lessor records the property as an asset and depreciates it over its useful life.

Operating leases allow organisations to treat leased assets as operating expenses rather than recording them on their balance sheets. However, recent changes to accounting standards under FRS16 mean that a right-of-use asset and a lease liability must be recorded on the organisation's balance sheet.

The effect of using equipment on an operating lease is to:

- Reduce the capital employed and therefore the target profit
- Reduce the company's financing costs
- Increase the operating costs by the amount of the lease payment.

A worked example of these effects can be seen in Appendix A.

3.5 Key Conclusions

3.5.1 Overall

This analysis in Appendix A suggests that operators outside London should be earning an operating profit margin of between **11.0%** and **15.0%** to earn a return in line with our estimate of the industry's current weighted average cost of capital (WACC), using current interest rates and dividend yields. This also makes allowance for the need to increase investment levels to meet decarbonisation targets and reduce the investment backlog. Should interest rates start to fall again, the size of the returns required will change in line. Modelling suggests that the target margins move by 0.4% for each 1% that interest rates change.

3.5.2 London Profits

Profit margins for bus operators are lower in London because the business model is completely different from the rest of the country: This can be seen from the figures in Appendix A. The differences include:

- Extensive use of operating leases radically alters the structure of the balance sheet
- Operating leases push borrowing and interest charges down, but increase operating costs
- Higher fuel consumption and much higher wages mean that operating costs in London are very much higher than they are in the rest of the country
- Vehicle operating days are longer and therefore more intensive use is made of assets, so that required returns represent a lower proportion of total income

The result is that the level of cash profits to meet target returns will be achieved at much lower profit margins. It is therefore completely misleading to read across from London profit margins to other parts of the deregulated world, and in franchised areas they will be dependent on the structure of the contract.

3.6 Actual Performance

It is possible to provide a rough outline of financial performance using the DfT's Annual Bus Statistics, which provide details of operator income and operating costs drawn from the annual STATS100 returns submitted by operators. Putting the two together provides an outline indication of profit performance. This can be done for each of the main industry sectors, though not at any more disaggregated level.

The result of the analysis for each year since 2009/10 for Great Britain outside London is shown in Table 10 below. The figures are adjusted for inflation to June 2023 prices by DfT using the GDP Deflator. It must be emphasised that these are a broad indication only and do not necessarily reflect the individual results of particular enterprises. Since they refer to local bus operations only, they will exclude other activities undertaken by operators, including contract work, coaching activities or engineering sales.

Table 10: Local Bus Service Earnings, 2010-2023, GB Outside London
£m, Constant (June 2023) Prices

Year to 31 March	Total Income	Operating Costs	Surplus/(Deficit)	Margin (%)
2010	5,716.6	4,828.4	888.2	15.5%
2011	5,608.2	4,753.2	855.0	15.2%
2012	5,578.5	4,839.5	739.0	13.2%
2013	5,473.6	4,778.4	695.2	12.7%
2014	5,406.3	4,761.2	645.1	11.9%
2015	5,256.3	4,720.9	535.3	10.2%
2016	5,232.3	4,687.5	544.7	10.4%
2017	5,114.0	4,584.2	529.8	10.4%
2018	5,083.6	4,469.8	613.9	12.1%
2019	5,037.0	4,570.9	466.1	9.3%
2020	4,747.2	4,519.4	227.9	4.8%
2021	4,406.4	3,941.7	464.7	10.5%
2022	4,172.4	4,375.0	(202.7)	(4.9%)
2023	4,274.8	4,217.8	57.0	1.3%

Source: PTIS Analysis of DfT Annual Bus Statistics, Sheets BUS04 and BUS05 plus data from Transport Scotland and Stats Wales.

It will be seen that the levels of surplus earned fell steadily over the period prior to Covid – this was partly driven by lower targets following reductions in the cost of capital after cuts in interest rates, but also by falls in earnings and service levels and increases in unit costs that were discussed in Chapters 1 and 2. Total income fell by £1.44 billion a year in real terms over the period (25%), whilst cost savings were limited to £611m (12.6%).

There was something of a boost to the surplus during the Covid year of 2020/21, as costs fell sharply during the lockdowns whilst operating income was maintained by government assistance. However, this was reversed in 2021/22 and barely recovered in 2022/23. The movement in margins is illustrated in Figure I below.

The margins for each sector for 2009/10 and 2022/23 are compared in Table 11 below, with more detailed information contained Appendix E. As can be seen, some sectors continued to record losses in 2022/23, the exception being Scotland, where a combination of the last tranche of post-Covid funding and the start of the Under 22 free travel scheme put operations back into the black.

Figure 1: Local Bus Operating Margins, 2010-2023, GB Outside London

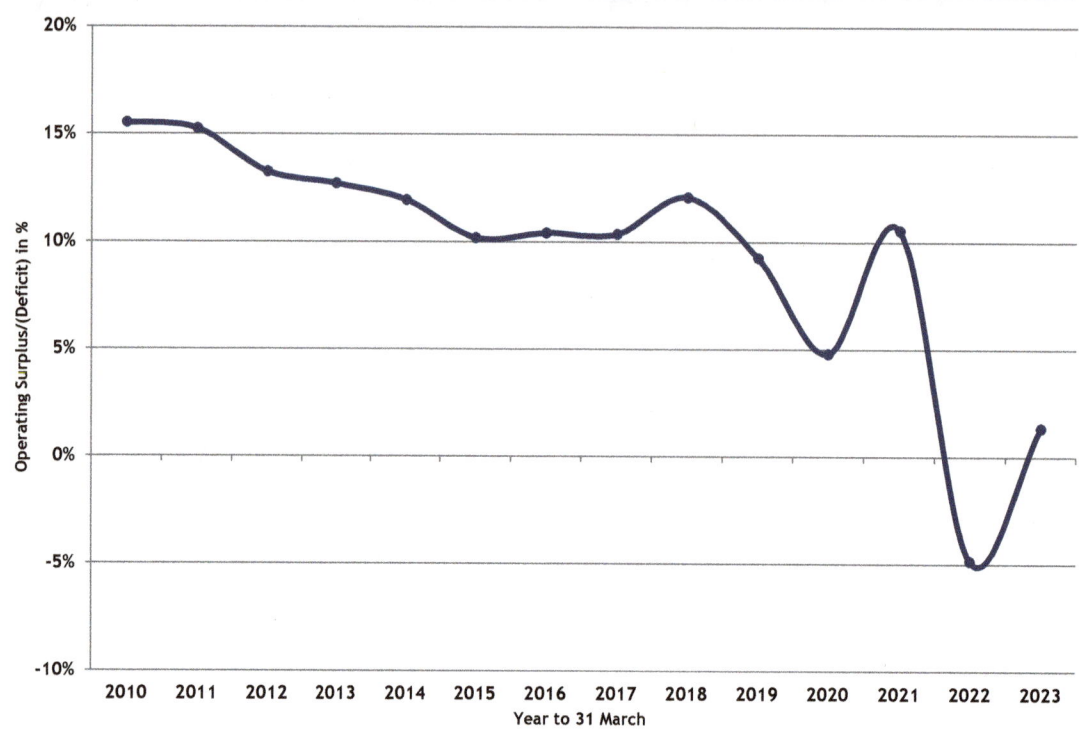

Table 11: Local Bus Operating Margins by Sector, 2009/10 v 2022/23

Year Ended 31 March	2023	2010
London	(2.7%)	4.2%
English Mets	(0.4%)	13.0%
English Shires	(0.3%)	15.8%
Scotland	10.0%	11.8%
Wales	(3.4%)	10.1%
GB Outside London	1.3%	14.0%

This page intentionally blank

Part B: Bus Regulation

Another Spin on the Regulatory Cycle?

Earlier this year, whilst researching a literature review for a client, I came across a fascinating paper by Professor Ken Gwilliam, presented at the 10th Thredbo conference in Sydney, Australia in 2008. The Thredbo series, or the *International Conference Series on Competition and Ownership in Land Passenger Transport* to give it is full title, started in 1989 and met every two years until Covid forced the postponement of the 2021 event for a year. The series is named for the Alpine village and ski resort at Thredbo, New South Wales, Australia, which was the venue for that first event in 1989. The 18th conference is scheduled to held in South Africa in the autumn of 2024.

Prof Gwilliam's paper was entitled *Bus Transport: is there a Regulatory Cycle?*[5]. As Professor of Transport Economics and Director of the Institute for Transport Studies from 1967 until 1988 and a visiting professor there for another twenty years, he could claim to have some expertise in the subject, especially having served as a non-executive director of the National Bus Company from 1978 until 1984.

Reviewing historic developments in both the industrialised and developing worlds, he suggested that there was a cycle which bus industries in various countries had previously gone through, which was an ongoing phenomenon. Reading his paper 16 years later, with another Labour government having recently taken office and promising more bus industry reform, his analysis seems very prescient.

His analysis of the cycle was represented by a diagram, which is reproduced Figure J below. Prof Gwilliam highlighted experience from several countries in order to reinforce his analysis, including the UK, and especially the experience between 1919 and 1949, which saw the bus market move through the cycle from the competitive private supply of the early 1920s to increasing consolidation and the involvement of the 'big four' railway companies from 1928 onwards to the local private sector monopolies delivered by the 1930 Road Traffic Act. Finally, the nationalisation of the 1947 Transport Act saw the a substantial proportion of operations move into the public sector – though the process was not finally complete until the acquisition of the private sector group British Electric Traction's substantial bus interests in 1967.

The cycle commenced again with the passage of the 1985 Transport Act, which was designed to break up the state monopolies and reduce the cost of subsidies to the Exchequer, objectives that were rapidly achieved, even if the hopes of reversing market decline were not fulfilled. The atomisation of the National Bus Company and later the Scottish Bus Group represented an attempt to ensure greater levels of competition between operators, but we can now see that the regulatory cycle began again with the re-consolidation of the industry into the five major groups between 1990 and 1997. On-the-road competition between operators – other than the incidental examples along shared corridors into town and city centres – had largely died out by the turn of the century, effectively establishing the private sector area monopolies, prompting new legislation to tighten regulation in 2000, 2008 and 2017. The result is the current position which, following the introduction of Enhanced Partnerships and Franchising, creates the

---

[5] *Available at:* https://thredbo-conference-series.org/papers/thredbo10/

regulated private monopolies that form stage three of the cycle. Now, in London, we see the first signs of re-nationalisation with Mayor Khan's plans to bring TfL bus operations back in house. On this basis, maybe we can expect the next era of deregulation to begin somewhere around 2050.

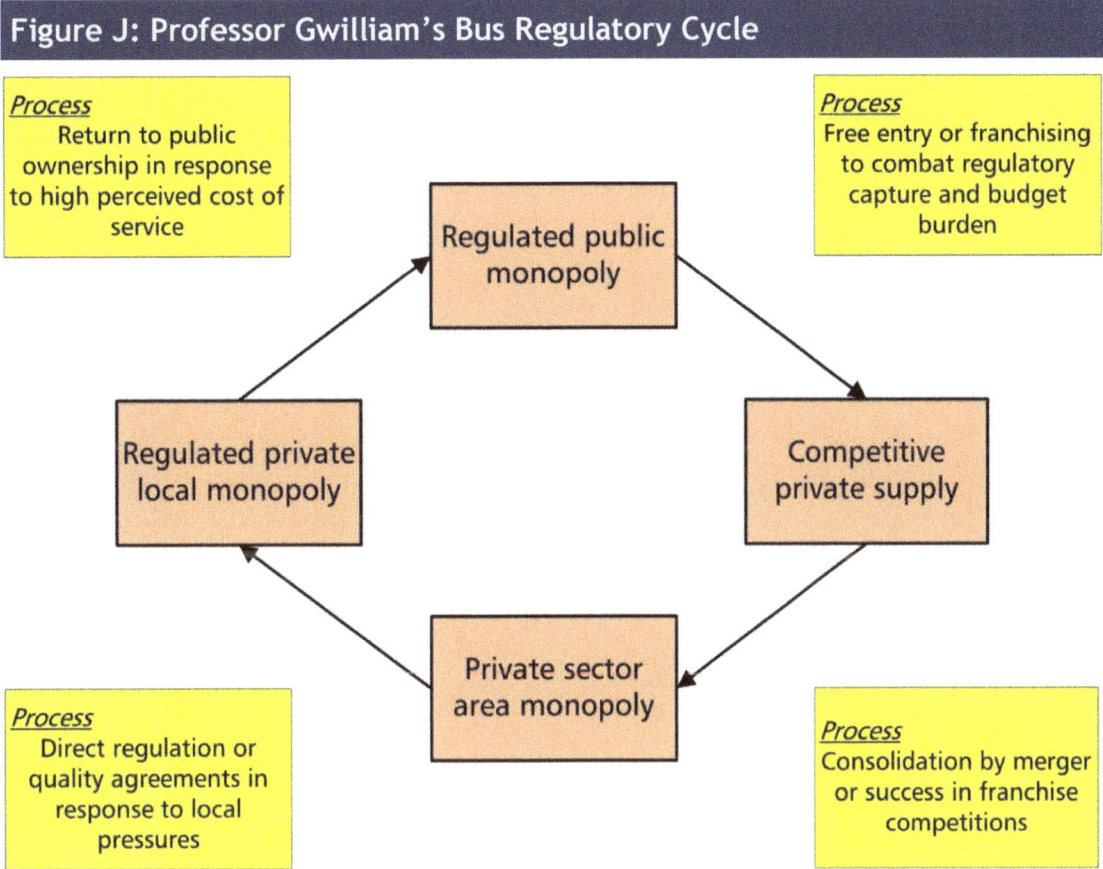

Figure J: Professor Gwilliam's Bus Regulatory Cycle

4. The National Bus Strategy and BSIPs

4.1 Introduction

The National Bus Strategy for England ('NBS') was published by the Department for Transport in March 2021.

It set out a vision and a strategy designed to transform the quality of bus services in England outside London, with the aim of making them more attractive, convenient, good value and popular for all to use. It argued that a successful bus service was good for the economy, for the environment, for the cost of living and for the quality of life in cities, towns and villages across the country.

DfT stated that locally driven change was central to delivery of the NBS, through new forms of partnership between the 80 local transport authorities (LTAs) in England outside London, bus operators and local stakeholders. The NBS stated that the Bus Services Act 2017 had provided the statutory framework need for the delivery of the strategy through partnership, requiring the parties in each area to develop a document setting out the vision, objectives and delivery plans of LTAs and their partners, known as a ***Bus Service Improvement Plan*** (BSIP).

The NBS stated explicitly that there could be no return to a post-deregulation model where bus services had been planned on a purely commercial basis with little or no engagement with, or support from, LTAs. BSIPs were to be the mechanism by which LTAs, working closely with their local bus operators and local communities, were to deliver incremental improvements in bus services.

NBS laid great emphasis on the topic of 'socially necessary' services, promising:

- new guidance on the meaning and role of 'socially necessary' services, which would "set clear expectations of what we want to see"
- expanding the category to include 'economically necessary' services for the first time, "recognising the vital role that buses have in getting people to work at all times of the day and night"
- provision for economically disadvantaged areas as part of the "levelling up" agenda.

As the strategy document put it: "Making sure that people are connected to centres of employment, broadening their choice of work and education, is both socially and economically important."

4.2 BSIP Delivery and Regulation

The delivery of a BSIP was made a condition for LTAs to continue to receive existing funding streams for buses, with the added incentive of a promise of further funding to deliver the practical measures needed to deliver the vision.

Initially, the LTAs were asked to make a choice by June 2021 between two options for future regulation of their bus networks, either a new form of statutory bus partnerships introduced in the 2017 Act, known as an Enhanced Partnership (EP) or bus service franchising. Of the 79 LTAs extant at the time[6], 76 opted to follow the EP route, and three expressed their intention to introduce franchising – Greater Manchester, Liverpool

---

[6] *The number has since increased to 80 with the creation of new unitary councils Cumberland and Westmoreland & Furness to replace Cumbria County Council.*

City Region and Cambridgeshire & Peterborough. Subsequently, five more Combined Authorities have said that they are assessing the franchising option. These are: North East, South Yorkshire, West Midlands, West of England and West Yorkshire. A further discussion on franchising can be found in Chapter 7 below.

Authorities were then set the challenge of developing their BSIPs by October 2021. The DfT's guidance on the structure and content of BSIPs, together with the collaborative process for producing them followed in May 2021, requiring the plans to be "well-evidenced, comprehensive and ambitious". In what the government afterwards called "an impressive achievement", all LTAs successfully produced a BSIP on time.

4.3 First Round Funding

The results of the BSIP assessment process undertaken by DfT were announced in April 2022, with the allocation of just over £1 billion of funding to 31 LTAs around the country. The authorities selected had received the money "because of their ambition to repeat the success achieved in London," reminding unsuccessful bidders of the NBS promise that areas not showing sufficient ambition, including for improvements to bus priority, would not be funded.

On increasing levels, the previous government had made a start on this, with the introduction in 2022 of Bus Service Improvement Plans and Enhanced Partnership Agreements. However, in the event, the funding was made available on a competitive basis, with just 30 out of 74 local transport authorities (LTAs) receiving funding for their plans, receiving a total allocation of £1.08 billion between them over the period 2022-2025.

4.4 Covid and BSIP+

Work on the NBS had started before the onset of the Covid-19 pandemic and was designed to build upon the levels and mode share existing in 2019. Afterwards, the mission became firstly to recover to 2019 levels and then move beyond.

Initially, funds to maintain bus services during Covid was provided centrally by DfT in a series of short-term support and recovery grant schemes totalling £3 billion. These were replaced in May 2023 by a new funding package designed to last from July 2023 until March 2025, at a total cost of £300m, including a £160m allocation to all LTAs to assist with the implementation of their improvement plans. This was initially known as BSIP+, then renamed BSIP Phase 2. A further £700m in BSIP funding was promised for local authorities in the North as part of the Network North announcement made following the decision to abandon Phase 2 of the HS2 project north of Birmingham.

4.5 Individual Allocations

The full listing of LTAs and the amounts they have been allocated by DfT can be seen in Appendix C below. The initial tranche saw £534m (49.3%) allocated to the Combined Authorities, with £296m (27.3%) to the remaining County Councils and £254m (23.4%) to the unitary authorities. In the BSIP+ allocations across the two years, £28m went to the Combined Authorities (17.8%), £69m (44.3%) to the counties and £60m (37.9%) to the unitary councils.

5. Enhanced Partnerships in England

5.1 Overview

At the time of writing, Enhanced Partnerships (EPs) are the preferred choice for all local transport authorities in England except the Combined Authorities. EPs were established under the Bus Services Act of 2017, initially one of three options that could be adopted by LTAs. As well as franchising, there was the 'Advanced Quality Partnership Scheme'. However, their use was effectively dropped by the NBS requirement for a binary choice between franchising and an EP.

A graphic outlining the process is provided in Figure K below. The diagram and the text which follows are drawn from the DfT's EP guidance documents[7].

An EP comprises two elements – an *EP Plan* and an *EP Scheme*.

5.2 The EP Plan

The EP Plan is a high-level strategic document based on BSIP content. It does not include details of specific actions or interventions, which are instead included in the EP Scheme (see below). Much of the work required will already be in the BSIP, so can be repeated in this document.

By law (Section 138A of the Transport Act 2000), each EP Plan must include:

- a map of the area it covers
- all the relevant factors that the parties consider will affect, or have the potential to affect, the local bus market over the life of the EP Plan
- a summary of information on passengers' experiences of using bus services in the area and their priorities for improvements.
- information on what measures would be required to encourage modal shift from car
- a summary of any available data on trends in bus journey speeds and the impact of congestion on local bus services
- the outcomes need to be delivered to improve local bus services in the EP Plan area
- what interventions the partnership believes necessary to deliver the outcomes.

In addition, the plan should include:

- the duration proposed
- proposals for the review of the EP Plan, including frequency and how and when the review is to happen. These can be different from the BSIP and the EP Scheme.
- an analysis of local bus services
- the objectives of the plan, including how bus service quality and effectiveness will be improved
- the policies regarding local bus services that will be pursued in the plan area

---

[7] *https://assets.publishing.service.gov.uk/government/uploads/system/uploads/attachment_data/file/1002507/national-bus-strategy.pdf*

- complementary policies on such issues as car parking and land use development
- how the related EP Scheme(s) are intended to assist in implementing the policies and achieving the objectives set out in the plan
- the intended effect of the EP Scheme(s) on neighbouring areas
- the LTA's proposals for consulting operators and passenger groups on how well the EP Plan and EP Scheme(s) are working.

Figure K: The Enhanced Partnership Process

```
Bus Service Improvement Plan
Choice: Franchise or Enhanced Partnership (EP)
  │
  ├── Franchise ──→ Start Franchising Process (see Chapter 7)
  │
  ↓ Enhanced Partnership

LTA prepares EP Plan with operators and stakeholders ──→ The EP Plan:
                                                          • Proposed duration
                                                          • Area covered
                                                          • Review factors determining demand
                                                          • Summary of Passenger Experiences
                                                          • Measures required to encourage modal shift from car
                                                          • Trends in bus speeds and congestion impacts
                                                          • Outcomes to be delivered
                                                          • Overview of interventions required
                                                          • Analysis of current network
                                                          • Plan objectives including how quality will be improved
                                                          • Policies to be pursued by LTA as regards bus services
                                                          • Complementary policies e.g. parking and land use
                                                          • How EP schemes will assist with the implementation of the Plan
  ↓

LTA prepares EP Scheme(s) ──→ The EP Scheme:
                              How policies set out in EP Plan will be delivered
                              • The scope of the scheme and commencement date
                              • Local Authority Obligations to deliver specified *facilities* and *measures*
                              • Bus Operator Obligations, including service standards such as vehicles, frequencies, ticketing, co-ordination
                              • The proposals for governance through an **EP Forum** including authorities, operators, passenger groups and stakeholders.
  ↓

OK to proceed? Operators Objection Period
  ├── NO ──→ Discuss Objections & Revise Proposals
  │            ├── RESOLVED ──→ (back to OK to proceed)
  │            └── UNRESOLVED ──→ Do not proceed
  ↓ YES

Public Consultation on Proposal ──→ The Consultees:
                                    • All affected bus operators
                                    • Passenger representatives
                                    • Neighbouring and lower tier local authorities
                                    • Traffic Commissioner and local police chief
                                    • Transport Focus
                                    • Competition and Markets Authority (CMA)
                                    • Such other persons as the authority thinks fit
  ↓

OK to proceed? Consultation Views
  ├── NO ──→ Discuss Objections & Revise Proposals
  ↓ YES

OK to proceed? Competition Tests
  ├── NO ──→ Discuss Objections & Revise Proposals
  ↓ YES

LTA adopts proposal, makes Plan & Scheme(s) ──→ Implementation
```

5.3 The EP Scheme(s)

The scheme document sets out the legal obligations on the relevant Local Authorities (including highway authorities) and local bus operators. It is the mechanism by which the commitments made in the BSIP and the EP Plan are delivered.

The scheme places an obligation:

a) on those authorities to deliver its requirements

b) on all bus operators to abide by the standards of service it imposes. Enforcement action can be taken by the registration authority if any bus operator fails to abide by such standards.

The EP Scheme document has to contain the following:

- the scope of the scheme and its commencement date
- local authority obligations
- bus operator obligations
- governance arrangements.

5.4 Local Authority Obligations

These can cover:

- Provision of facilities, including for example:
    - New and existing bus lanes (potentially including hours of operation)
    - New and existing bus gates
    - Pedestrian crossing upgrades
    - Traffic signal upgrades
    - New bus stop/stand infrastructure
    - Real-time information displays
    - Hydrogen refuelling facilities.
- Measures, including:
    - Bus lane enforcement
    - Management of roadworks
    - Applying a fare subsidy (subject to operator agreement)

5.5 Bus Operator Obligations

These can cover:

- Vehicle standards and facilities
- Timetable change dates
- Ticketing facilities and products
- Multi-operator ticketing prices
- Frequency enhancements
- Frequency limitations
- Headway requirements
- Timetable co-ordination, including with other modes

5.6 Governance Arrangements

Governance of the EP Plan and EP Scheme(s) is in the hands of body known as a Forum. This body controls the future content of and the arrangements for the variation or revocation of the EP Plan and EP Scheme(s). Guidance says that the membership of the Forum should include all the key stakeholders responsible for the content of the documents. The bodies represented should be:

- the LTAs and relevant lower-tier authorities that will be delivering the EP Scheme
- bus operators providing local bus services.
- other organisations that have agreed to take part such as:
  - passenger representatives
  - disability groups
  - local businesses

Allowance is to be made for guest attendees. The documentation should include practical arrangements, such as the frequency and location of forum meetings, the decision-making process, and administrative arrangements. Arrangements for adding new (non-statutory) members and for the handling of the operator objection mechanism (see below) also need to be set out.

5.7 Operator Objections

Once the draft EP Plan and EP Scheme have been published, operators of registered local bus services in the area(s) covered by the proposals may object, in writing, within 28 days of the publication. Any objections lodged must be published by the LTA. Depending on the number of objectors and the share of local service mileage they operate, the objections can prevent the plan and/or the scheme from proceeding to consultation until the objections are resolved.

5.8 Consultation

The consultation process is required, as a minimum to cover statutory consultees. These are:

- all operators of local bus services that would be affected by any of the proposals
- organisations that represent local passengers
- other local authorities that would be affected by the proposals
- the relevant Traffic Commissioner
- the chief officer of police for each area to which the plan relates
- Transport Focus
- the Competition and Markets Authority (CMA)

The authority may also consult such other persons as it thinks fit.

Once the consultation has been concluded, the authority must decide whether any of the representations received require modification of the EP Plan or EP Scheme(s). If so, the changes may trigger the operator objection provisions again. However, the hope is that, having worked in partnership with operators and other stakeholders throughout the process of developing the BSIP and the EP proposals, this should not be necessary.

5.9 EPs and Competition Law

Within an enhanced partnership, the power of decision-making as to whether to operate a service or not remains a commercial judgement for the bus operator, provided that they meet the service standards laid down in the EP documentation.

As the DfT guidance[8] puts it:

> "The CMA recognises that passengers can benefit from effective partnerships between bus operators and LTAs. Such beneficial forms of cooperation can include better integrated networks, multi-operator ticketing schemes, integrated information management and marketing. Although the perceived threat of CMA action still remains a significant barrier to closer partnership working, the CMA does not want LTAs or bus operators to be deterred from introducing partnership arrangements that benefit customers but do not weaken rivalry between operators by unfounded concerns that they might breach competition law."

An EP Scheme imposes legal requirements on operators of local bus services using the 'standards of service' that it applies. Obeying these legal requirements does not breach competition law for the operators concerned – even if it involves actions that might otherwise do so, such as joint-working on timetabling.

The guidance notes that LTA coordination of network planning does not inherently raise competition concerns provided that the authority works in partnership with local bus operators to build on their normal business practice of conducting network reviews and uses the EP mechanisms set out in the legislation. However, a planned bus network does not require competition between operators to be eliminated.

The Competition Tests

The two tests agreed originally in 2000 as part of the passage of the Transport Act 2000 remain in place, and LTAs and operators are urged to pay due regard to these in delivering their EPs.

Part 1 Test

Making or varying an Enhanced Partnerships and any multi-operator ticketing scheme that is a part of them, are subject to the test in Part 1 of Schedule 10 to the Transport Act 2000. This test has three elements:

a) Is there likely to be a significantly adverse effect on competition? If yes:

b) Is the exercise of the function being done with a view to securing one or more of the three purposes specified (known as 'bus improvement objectives'), either:

- to secure improvements in the quality of vehicles or facilities used to provide local services
- to secure other improvements in local services of benefit to users of local services, or
- to reduce or limit traffic congestion, noise or air pollution; and

---

[8] *The Bus Services Act 2017: Enhanced Partnerships. Accessed via*
https://assets.publishing.service.gov.uk/government/uploads/system/uploads/attachment_data/file/1002507/national-bus-strategy.pdf

c) Is the effect on competition proportionate or likely to be proportionate to the achievement of that purpose?

As these objectives are at the core of the BSIP developed jointly with operators, the DfT states that they would expect them to be satisfied but advises that they should still be assessed on a case-by-case basis.

Part 2 Test

The Part 2 test is required where there is an agreement between bus undertakings (called a qualifying agreement) which 'has as its object or effect the prevention, restriction or distortion of competition in the area of the authority, or the combined area of the authorities'.

Where such arrangements 'prevent, restrict or distort competition' they are allowed if certain requirements are satisfied. Such agreements must be certified by the LTA on the following basis:

a) the agreement must be in the interests of passengers using local services in the area of the local authority/ies concerned

b) it must not impose on the undertakings concerned restrictions that are not indispensable to the attainment of the bus improvement objectives (in this case compliance with the relevant route requirement).

In addition, the agreement:

- must contribute to the attainment of one or more of the bus improvement objectives
- must not impose on the undertakings concerned restrictions which are not indispensable to the attainment of those objectives, and
- must not afford the undertakings concerned the possibility of eliminating competition in respect of a substantial part of the services in question.

Again, the guidance states that, if such an agreement is required to deliver BSIP outcomes the DfT would expect these tests to be met but they need to be considered on a case by case basis.

5.10   Criticisms of the EP Process

There is no doubt that negotiating, establishing and maintaining an EP takes time and resources that neither operators nor LTAs really have. This was highlighted in a report reviewing the operation of the 2017 Bus Services Act, published by the Local Government Association (LGA) and the Urban Transport Group (UTG) in 2023. They suggested that there were weaknesses in the EP regime and called for consideration to be given to simplifying the process[9]. Their ideas may form part of the new Government's planned Better Buses Bill.

In particular, the report highlights the objection procedures, stating "it remains open to question as to how far a mechanism that permits all incumbents to pursue their self-interests can simultaneously deliver the step-change required in service delivery, fares and

---

[9] *A Smoother Ride: Reviewing the Bus Services Act 2017 to empower local areas. Urban Transport Group and Local Government Association, September 2023.* https://urbantransportgroup.org/system/files/general-docs/UTG%20Report%20-%20A%20Smoother%20Ride%20FINAL_2.pdf

other passenger benefits." As a result, the report states, some LTAs find it a struggle to realise any 'enhanced' outputs from EPs, especially those not linked to funding.

As a result, the report recommends that changes should be made to "derisk" the EP process, reviewing the objection thresholds so that they are not used unreasonably to stop authorities and groups of operators progressing EPs, adding that "Objection thresholds should be set at levels which allow for valid objection, but do not allow for small groups of operators (particularly larger operators) to block an otherwise effective EP."

A second concern is the role of the competition authorities, discussed in section 5.9 above. LGA and UTG note that the Competition and Markets Authority (CMA) is a statutory consultee on EP Plans and EP Schemes and that they can launch an investigation if they consider that the proposals do not meet the competition test(s). However, in guidance published on May 2023, CMA stated that it could not "provide legal assurances on whether schemes and plans comply with competition law. It is for LTAs to apply the Test and make any relevant competition law assessment themselves." The report suggests that such a risk may deter authorities from pursuing bolder changes to fares and ticketing.

The report states that these issues, alongside the question of whether funding is sufficient, call into question the ability to transform bus networks in the way envisaged by the National Bus Strategy – and calls for an urgent review of whether EPs are delivering.

6. Bus Service Improvement Partnerships in Scotland

6.1 Origins and Legislation

Bus Service Improvement Partnerships were introduced under the Transport (Scotland) Act 2019 as a replacement for the Statutory Quality Partnerships originally introduced in the 2001 Act. Some associated regulations were passed in 2023, but further sets were awaited, along with detailed guidance on BSIP implementation, at the time of writing.

The Act sets out the planned process, including the fact that BSIPs will be made by the LTA(s), and will be overseen by the Traffic Commissioner. The plans are intended to be "collaborative partnerships which will have analysed the existing service provision in the area and the policies to be implemented, in order to make substantive improvements and achieve those policies"[10].

As in England, the Scottish BSIP process draws a distinction between a **_BSIP Plan_** and a **_BSIP Scheme_**. An illustration of the process as currently understood can be found in Figure L below.

6.2 The BSIP Plan

The Act lays down that the BSIP Plan must:

- Specify the area covered and time period to which it relates
- Provide an analysis of local services
- Specify policies relating to local services
- Set out:
  - objectives on quality and effectiveness of local services
  - how the scheme will meet these objectives
  - the intended effect of any partnership scheme on adjacent areas
  - how and when the partnership plan will be reviewed.
- Specify how the views of users are to be obtained on the effectiveness of plan and scheme

6.3 BSIP Partnership Scheme

To accompany the BSIP Plan, LTAs are required to make one or more BSIP Schemes relating to the whole or a part of the area specified in the Plan. A scheme needs to specify:

- the area covered by the scheme and period of time
- the service standards for services having one or more stopping places in the area
- the facilities to be provided by the LTA (i.e. infrastructure)
- the measures to be taken by the LTA, such as parking policy, to incentivise bus use.
- how and when the scheme will be reviewed

---

[10] *Bus Service Improvement Partnerships (BSIPs), Transport Scotland.*
https://www.transport.gov.scot/media/48594/bus-service-improvement-partnerships-note.pdf

Figure L: Bus Service Improvement Partnerships: The Process

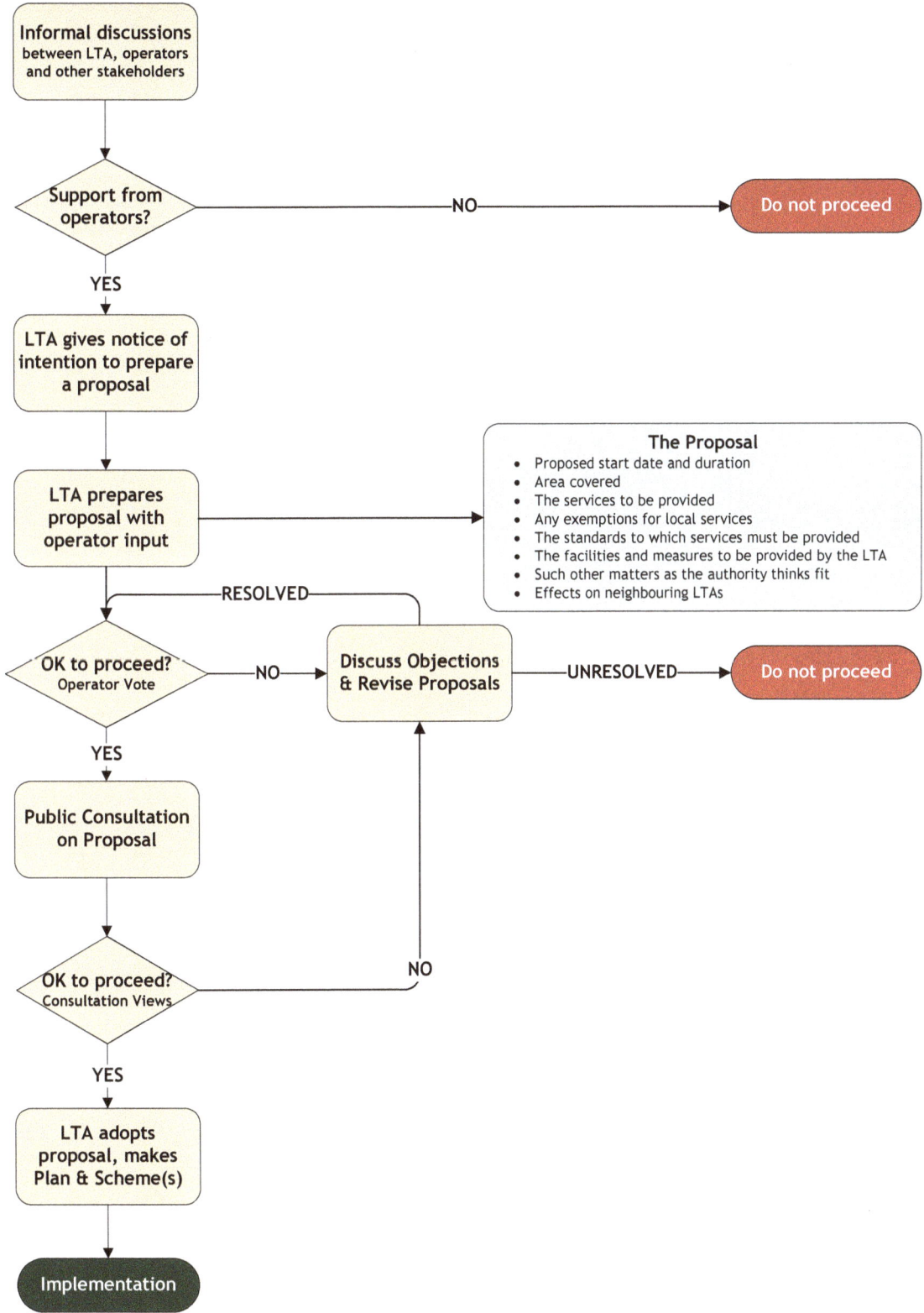

Reporting Progress

There is a requirement for the LTA to prepare and publish an annual report on the effectiveness of the scheme for each year the scheme is in effect. The report is required to consider all representations made to the LTA. The Traffic Commissioner must be consulted, as they will have powers to call LTAs as well as operators to account for non-implementation of their obligations under the BSIP.

It is envisaged that the Scheme may:

- provide for exemption of services and conditions in which such exemptions are to apply
- specify actions to facilitate the operation of the scheme
- provide for circumstances where the scheme can be varied or revoked

The scheme can only be made:

- if the LTA is satisfied it will contribute to implementation of the policies set out in the BSIP plan or other relevant general policies and
- it will bring benefits to users or reduce or limit congestion, noise or air pollution

6.4 Bus Operator Obligations

Subject to detailed regulations and guidance, the service standards required of operators may include:

- route service standards: requirements on the frequency or timing of a local service, either singly or in conjunction with others
- operational service standards: any other matter relating to standard of service, including (but not limited to):
  - vehicle quality specifications
  - minimum frequency of services
  - maximum frequency of services
  - maximum fares
  - ticketing requirements
  - multi-operator travel card pricing
  - provision of information for the public
  - dates of registration changes.

7. Bus Franchising

7.1 Introduction

The initial legislation on "franchising" came in the form of two Transport Acts, in England in 2000 and Scotland in 2001, which introduced the concept of a "Quality Contract" (QC). To quote the House of Commons Library[11]: "Under a Contract scheme, the local authority determines what local services should be provided in the area concerned (including the routes, the timetable and the fares) and lets contracts with bus operators, granting them exclusive rights to provide services to the authority's specification. The authority may make payments to the provider of the services and either party may be required to provide additional features or services."

It is this exclusivity that distinguishes QCs or "franchises" from partnerships, which by law must be available to all local bus operators who meet the standards set out in the partnership agreement.

In England and Wales, the QC provisions were updated in the Local Transport Act 2008, which, amongst other things, replaced the requirement for the Secretary of State's approval with an expert panel chaired and appointed by the local Traffic Commissioner. Further changes were made for England in the Bus Services Act 2017 – the latter granting extensive powers to devolved Mayors in Combined Authority areas without the need for oversight by the Secretary of State or the Traffic Commissioner.

In Scotland, the powers granted under the 2001 Act were never used and were replaced in the Transport (Scotland) Act 2019 by new powers for "Local Services Franchises". The powers came into effect on 4 December 2023, but detailed regulations and guidance on this aspect of the Act were still awaited at the time of writing. The Act shows that the process for introducing these is complex, and the need for approval by an expert panel convened by the Traffic Commissioner mirrors the provisions of the 2008 Act in England, which were abolished there in 2017 after the failure of the Tyne and Wear QC attempt. So far, one Scottish authority, the Strathclyde Partnership for Transport (SPT) has indicated a wish to move towards franchising, in a programme expected to take between five and seven years to implement and cost around £15m to complete.

In Wales, legislation was at the time of writing promised "imminently" to deliver the Welsh Government's ambition to introduce a country-wide franchising system, as included in their White Paper *One Network, One Timetable, One Ticket: Planning Buses as a Public Service for Wales*, published in March 2022[12]. This was confirmed in a new document, *Our Roadmap to Bus Reform, Towards One Network, One Timetable, One Ticket*, published in March 2024[13]

In all three cases, the new powers are not overly prescriptive, and within the 'franchising' principle, a number of different operating models and *modus operandi* have emerged even within the broad definition set out above. This is discussed further in section 7.3 below.

---

[11] *Buses: Franchising. House of Commons Library, Standard Note SN624. 19 April 2012.*
[12] *https://www.gov.wales/one-network-one-timetable-one-ticket-planning-buses-public-service-wales-html*
[13] *https://www.gov.wales/sites/default/files/publications/2024-03/march-2024-our-roadmap-to-bus-reform.pdf*

7.2 An International Perspective

7.2.1 The Thredbo Series

As noted above, the Thredbo series of international conferences has since 1989 focused on competition and ownership in land passenger transport[14].

The 17th conference was held in September 2022 and featured a series of workshops to discuss key policy issues[15]. Reviewing the conclusions, a number seem to be of relevance to future of policymaking in the UK:

- Success requires trust between politicians, transport authority officers and operators through clear mandates, common interests and appropriate investments of time

- All the main stakeholders need to be genuinely involved in the design of tender (or other selection) processes and of service contracts. This especially includes potential operators who are expected to price, bid, fulfil contracts and carry risk; and representatives of labour, who may be impacted by transition and then over the contract life.

- Barriers to participation in competitive tendering need to be lowered. Traditional procurement processes tend to be expensive and time-consuming, and often not friendly for participants. Processes need to be streamlined, more intuitive and avoid unnecessary burdens on bidders.

- Greater attention must be paid to how innovation is dealt with in tendering processes and in contracts. The openness, flexibility and management of risk required for innovation do not sit well with standard public procurement and the associated contracts.

- The core policy objective must always be to grow public transport usage. Social objectives need to be balanced with this core policy objective. This can be discussed from different perspectives, such as fare strategies, and social obligation.

In an earlier conference, Van den Velde (1997)[16] argued that a more structured view of planning and control was required in the planning and development of contracts. As with other economic activities decisions in public transport provision could be ordered hierarchically, depending on the time horizons and the scope of the issues. This approach could link three levels of decision-making, the strategic, the tactical and the operational. He suggested that this came down to three questions:

- What are we trying to achieve? A strategic decision on general aims and broad definition of how to achieve them

- What product can help to achieve the aims? Decisions on the means by which the aims can be reached, and how to use those aims most efficiently.

- How do we produce the product? Make sure the decisions are implemented in an efficient way.

Van den Velde (1997) presented this analysis in the form of a table, reproduced as Table 12 below.

---

[14] https://thredbo-conference-series.org/
[15] https://thredbo-conference-series.org/papers/thredbo17/Thredbo-17-Key-Policy-Document.pdf
[16] *Entrepreneurship and Tendering in Local Public Transport Services*, Prof. D M Van der Velde, 6th Thredbo Conference, 1997.

Table 12: Levels of Planning and Control in Public Transport

Decision level	General description	Decisions	
STRATEGIC Long term (5 years)	What do we want to achieve?	General Aims<ul><li>Transport policy</li><li>Market share</li><li>Profitability</li></ul>General Service Characteristics<ul><li>Areas</li><li>Target groups</li><li>Intermodality</li></ul>	
TACTICAL Medium term (1-2 years)	Which services can help to achieve these aims?	Detailed service characteristics	
		"Software"<ul><li>Fares</li><li>Image</li><li>Additional Services</li></ul>	"Hardware"<ul><li>Vehicles</li><li>Routes</li><li>Timetables</li></ul>
OPERATIONAL Short term (1-6 months)	How to produce these services?	Sales<ul><li>Selling activities</li><li>Information to the public</li></ul>	Production<ul><li>Infrastructure management</li><li>Vehicle rostering & maintenance</li><li>Personnel rostering and management</li></ul>

7.2.2 The OECD International Transport Forum

The role of buses in helping to deliver an enhanced quality of life, with net-zero emissions, and improved opportunities for all people is growing in importance for many social, demographic and environmental reasons.

In 2020, a working group established under the auspices of the International Transport Forum produced a report[17] about how to reform public transport planning and delivery to meet these growing needs. The group noted that the broader policy context, including the liveability of cities, was becoming relatively more important than controlling the costs of public transport. As a result, they recommended:

- Decentralised tiers of government should take the lead role planning public transport services to ensure that the needs of all local people and places were included. There were, however, risks from too much decentralisation, because:
  - administrative boundaries were not necessarily aligned with the transport planning boundaries – for example, travel to work areas, etc. This risked a lack of co-ordination and integration

---

[17] OECD/ITF 2020 Reforming Public Transport Planning and Delivery.
https://www.oecd.org/content/dam/oecd/en/publications/reports/2020/08/reforming-public-transport-planning-and-delivery_6f24c0d3/6c2f1869-en.pdf

- - a disconnect could arise in planning between local objectives and the policies and priorities set by national governments.
- The system should be designed to ensure the existence of a competitive market for contracts which could be sustained and developed over time.
- As part of this, careful consideration needed to be given to the length and size of contracts, avoiding concessions that were too large. Contract lengths needed to be set so that investment expenditures could be amortised and contractors could gain expertise in serving the relevant market(s).
- System operation should be separated from the ownership of the main assets such as vehicles and depots. This could reduce barriers to entry and increase the number of bidders for contracts.
- Quality standards should be linked to both inputs (e.g. quality of information provision, regular maintenance and fleet renewal) and outputs (e.g. punctuality, passenger satisfaction). Given the importance of service quality to the delivery of a sustainable public transport system, operator incentives should be aligned with performance standards and be large enough to be effective.
- Transparency and accountability were essential to the achievement of a successful privately operated, publicly regulated system. A trusting relationship made contract negotiation (and re-negotiation to address changes in the environment) smoother and less costly.
- Authorities must focus on service quality, including the integration of the public transport offer, to improve such matters as reliability, regularity and frequency. Contracts should be designed to offer incentives for better service.
- Authorities should engage positively with providers of shared mobility services and micro-mobility services in order to maximise complementarities with traditional public transport, especially in the context of developments on Mobility as a Service (MaaS).

The report also stated that converting publicly owned transport operators into incorporated companies could achieve cost savings and service quality improvements but was not a reform strategy in itself.

7.2.3 The New Zealand Experience

International experience has provided much material for researchers and academics in public transport reform that has moved operations from publicly owned and operated models to publicly controlled but privately operated networks or even the deregulated model adopted in parts of the UK. However, there has been little experience of moving in the opposite direction.

This was pointed out in a paper reviewing the prospects for bus franchising by Villa.i.Aguilar, Rye, Cowie and McTigue (2022)[18] who went on to examine the experience in New Zealand, the only country which did take that step.

---

[18] Bus franchising in English and Scottish regions - Viable solution or unfeasible instrument? *Villa.i.Aguilar Xavier, Rye Tom, Cowie Jonathan, and McTigue Clare. Journal of Transport Policy, Vol 120, May 2022.*
https://www.napier.ac.uk/-/media/worktribe/output-2847399/bus-franchising-in-english-and-scottish-regions--viable-solution-or-unfeasible.ashx

New Zealand liberalised its bus regulation along UK lines in the 1980s, with abolition of quantity licensing in 1983. This was followed by a series of Acts of Parliament to liberalise the wider economy[19], reforming industrial relations, local content legislation and the way the public sector operated. The State Owned Enterprise Act of 1986 turned parts of central government that could be expected to trade as commercial entities into "arm's length" bodies. This included NZ Rail, which had hitherto dominated the bus and coach industry.

Further legislation - the Transport Services Licensing Act 1989 – opened up the entire transport industry for competition, including bus services in the main urban areas. The four local authorities with bus operations – Wellington, Auckland, Christchurch and Dunedin – all turned their bus operations into arms-length companies. Wellington City Transport was sold to Stagecoach in 1992, followed by Auckland in 1998. The two were later sold on by Stagecoach, and formed the backbone of NZ Bus, now owned by Australian bus group Kinetic, co-owners since 2021 of the UK's Go-Ahead Group.

The 1980s reforms were not judged to have been a success and patronage continued to fall, requiring additional public support to maintain the network. In an atmosphere of disagreement between operators and regional councils, the government decided to legislate and passed the Public Transport Management Act of 2008, with further control introduced with the Public Transport Operating Model (PTOM) in 2013.

PTOM saw the introduction of fully contracted bus services. Introduced in 2013, this involved a mix of competitively tendered and negotiated bus contracts[20] in the main metropolitan areas. Wallis (2020)[21] reports the key features of the PTOM were as follows:

- Adoption of a partnering approach to service planning and delivery, recognising that operators and authorities are both stakeholders, and rely on each other. This was to be achieved by mechanisms such as collaborative business planning, joint investments, and financial incentives

- All services would be specified by regional councils, with the previous distinction between commercial and subsidised services being abolished apart from a few services outside the region's core network.

- Contracts were bundled into "units" comprising several routes or groups of routes, designed to be both logical from a customer point of view and attractive to potential bidders.

- All contracts were to let on a gross cost basis in order to facilitate service planning and integrated fares and ticketing systems.

- All main assets (buses, depots) were to be provided by operators. This was in line with previous NZ practice.

The default position was that all contracts would be subject to competitive tender. Two exceptions were made, however, which are worthy of note:

---

[19] *"Our History" The Bus & Coach Association New Zealand.* https://busandcoach.co.nz/about-us/history/.
[20] *Negotiated contracts are also known as Direct Awards, a system used in Europe and deployed in the UK in recent passenger rail contracts and for several years with Translink, Northern Ireland's publicly owned rail and bus operator.*
[21] *Wallis, Ian, Ian Wallis Associates. Value for Money in Procurement of Urban Bus Services -- Competitive Tendering versus Negotiated Contracts: Recent New Zealand Experience. August 2020.*
https://ses.library.usyd.edu.au/bitstream/handle/2123/27185/Value%20for%20Money%20in%20Procurement%20of%20Urban%20Bus%20Services.pdf?sequence=1&isAllowed=n

- Contracts could be negotiated in exchange for commercial services previously operated in the region, on a 'like-for-like' basis. Thus, if an operator had previously been running x bus kilometres a year in the region on commercial services, they were entitled to negotiate contracts covering an equal number of bus kilometres

- At the discretion of the regional council, other units in the main centres with relatively high cost recovery ratios could be awarded by negotiation.

The procurement process was as follows:

- An initial invitation to tender was issued either on an 'open' or a 'closed' basis with respondents submitting bids and other proposed operating details.

- The 'open' contract bids were evaluated first, so establishing a benchmark for costs, which was used by the tendering authorities in the discussions for the negotiated contracts.

- Whilst this process was successful in smoothing the transition from a deregulated to a regulated system, analysis of the tender price outcome by Wallis (2020) showed that negotiated contract prices were between 10% and 15% higher than tendered prices in Auckland and 30-35% higher in Wellington.

- The requirement for tendering authorities to negotiate "like for like" contracts with some operators weakened their negotiating position, and there was no option to revert to competitive tendering. At the same time, Wallis notes that a committed timetable for the transition to PTOM left the councils with a deadline by which agreement had to be reached, again weakening their negotiating position.

7.2.4 The Jersey Experience[22]

The States of Jersey regulated its bus network for the first time in 2002, developing a gross cost contract for a ten year period, which was awarded to a French operator, Connex (later Veolia Transport, now part of Transdev). The contract was held to have been successful in delivering a robust, reliable network and a fleet of new vehicles for the service.

However, the gross cost model proved to have two disadvantages:

- There was no incentive to reduce unit costs through innovation – or even to have a close interest in cost control.

- There was no incentive for the operator to deploy entrepreneurial skills and experience in network design, scheduling, ticketing, marketing etc since all incremental revenue goes to the contracting authority and not the operator.

- This latter point was considered crucial, since the States needed to find an affordable way to improve and increase bus service provision and patronage to meet the targets in its Sustainable Transport Policy document, issued in 2010.

With the assistance of consultants, new proposals were drawn up. In summary form, the process was:

- Pre-qualified bidders were invited to bid against a 'model network' to provide a consistent base price

---

[22] *This account is a precis of a document, Practical Bus Franchising: the Jersey Model, published by HCT Group with the States of Jersey, 2016. https://democracy.leeds.gov.uk/documents/s144378/app3%20hct%20group.pdf*

- Two finalists were then selected and invited to propose their own network designs which met the requirements of the States but offered better services or enhanced efficiency
- The network proposed by the winner and agreed by the States became the "reference network" which the government commissioned.

The contract contained several important provisions, including:

- Shared risks, with a minimum subsidy contract. The States are obliged to subsidise the operator if the fare revenue falls below the costs of operation, but the operator shares any revenue upside with the States above a certain level
- An initial seven year period, with the possibility of extensions depending on performance at trigger points during the contract (designed to avoid mid or late contract complacency)
- Specification of smart ticketing and trackable vehicles, plus open book accounting allowing government access to patronage data and full cost data
- Consultation on network changes and/or enhancements with both government and passengers
- A fail-safe mechanism, allowing the States to step in in the event of service or organisational failure.

The contract was let in 2013, and by 2016 was successful in delivering 32% more passengers, enhanced customer satisfaction, cost savings and several network enhancements. The operation was let to HCT Group, who held the contract until 2022, when the business was sold to the Australian Kelsian Group, at that time co-proprietors of London bus company RATP Dev Transit London. The States of Jersey currently plans to let a new contract for the island's bus services commencing in 2025.

7.3 Franchise Architecture

Even within the principle of franchising in the current legislation, many key decisions about the form and nature of the contracts are left open. These cover such issues as governance, asset purchase, and vehicle provision. The following sections discuss some of these and examine possible alternative models /methodologies.

7.3.1 The Gross Cost Model

The London and Greater Manchester schemes operate on a gross cost model. Key features include:

- full commercial risk for the tendering authorities, including network planning, marking and promotion, fares and ticketing and income
- full costs of operation plus a profit margin paid by authority to operator regardless of network commercial performance
- no operator incentive for revenue or patronage growth unless specific incentives are built into the contract
- attribution of risks is required, especially on revenue and cost variations (e.g. inflation levels and cost variations as well as external disruptions to services and *force majeure* events,) over the life of the contract.

7.3.2 The Net Cost Model

A possible alternative model might be what is termed a "minimum subsidy" or "net cost" contract. This has operated successfully in Jersey for a number of years, and was tried in London in the mid-1990s, before being abandoned as giving the authority "too little control".

Features might include:

- Operators bid for a service level agreement on a 'reference network'
- Shared commercial risk between operator and authorities
- Operator receives reimbursement of costs only if they are not covered by revenue
- Operator incentivised to grow revenue and patronage
- Operator may be free to operate additional services within the reference area at their own risk
- Full open book accounting, with tendering authority entitled to a profit share beyond an agreed level.

7.3.3 Contract Design

There are a number of different approaches as to how franchised bus networks might be organised. There are two basic approaches:

- Route franchises: contracts let by individual routes or small groups of interlinked routes (as London). These are particularly well-suited to rural areas and for maximising opportunities for SMEs in other areas
- Network franchises: contracts let covering a network of routes in a defined geographical area which can cover specific corridors, the operations undertaken by a specific depot or, more widely, a local authority area. The latter is the model generally used in France, where the tendering authorities tend to let whole networks to one operator.

7.3.4 Asset ownership

There are two basic models for asset ownership under a franchising system:

- Authority-owned land, buildings and other equipment, let to the operator as part of a contract. This model is usually associated with a network franchise and can reduce operator capital employed and therefore the level of profit needed by the operator. There is an upfront capital cost to the tendering authority – and the authority needs to meet its ongoing financial obligations on asset ownership
- Operator-owned assets for the running of the service(s), the cost of which is reimbursed by the authority as part of the contract. This reduces the upfront cost to the tendering authority but increases operator capital employed and therefore profit needed by operator to meet their financial obligations.

Both arrangements would be subject to negotiation on responsibilities, residual values, capture of unexpired value of long-term investments made part way through a contract, etc. In the initial letting of the contract and in subsequent renewals, the authority can assist or even participate in negotiations over the transfer of land and building assets between the incumbent commercial operator and authority (if funds are available) or, in the case of contract re-letting, from one operator to another.

7.3.5 Vehicle Provision

Similarly, there are options available for the provision of the buses needed to operate the services.

- The tendering authority acquires vehicles by purchase or operating lease, provides them to the operator for a fee that forms part of the contract
  - The tendering authority takes residual value risk
  - The public sector can generally borrow on more advantageous terms than the private, but expenditure may be subject to the authority's borrowing limits
  - This option reduces operator capital employed and therefore profit needed by operator.
- Alternatively, the operator acquires vehicles by purchase or operating lease, provides them to the authority as part of the contract (as in London)
  - The attribution of residual value risks require negotiation. Terms would be dependent on length of contract. Arrangements would need to be in place for vehicles which are not life-expired at the end of a contract. Some form of purchase guarantee could be negotiated so that either the tendering authority or the successor operator purchases the vehicles on contract expiry. Alternatively, residual value risk could be left with the original operator, but this would be priced into the initial contract and there would be a risk of disruption at the handover date if new vehicles had then to be acquired.
  - This option would increase operator capital employed and therefore profit needed by operator to meet financial obligations.

7.3.6 Franchise Governance

Thus far, the question of what level of authority is responsible for a bus franchise has not been an issue in England, with the mayoral combined authorities (MCAs) being given the power to introduce them under the 2017 Bus Services Act, and the MCAs being the Local Transport Authority (LTA) for their area. A complication arises where the powers of the Highway Authority remain with borough councils.

Going forward, many LTAs in England are currently too small to contemplate franchising, whilst in Scotland and Wales, the position remains unclear – in both cases, the current unitary authority is also the LTA. However, elsewhere there is an intermediate level of local government (the Regional Transport Partnerships (RTPs) in Scotland and the four Corporate Joint Committees (CJCs) in Wales) and both devolved governments have their own transport agencies in Transport Scotland and Transport for Wales.

In Scotland, the 2019 Act places the decisions as to whether and how to use the powers granted over bus services to the LTAs and the RTPs. In Wales, however, the current plan, as set out in *Our Roadmap to Bus Reform*, published in March 2024, is that "decisions about bus services in Wales (including routes, timetables, fares, hours of operation and service quality standards) will be made by Welsh Government and Transport for Wales". However, it adds that "decisions will be made in partnership with Corporate Joint Committees".

7.4 Implementation

As discussed in section 7.1 above, the procedures for implementing a franchise were updated by the Bus Services Act 2017 in England and the Transport (Scotland) Act 2019 in Scotland. Legislation for Wales was expected shortly at the time of writing.

The two pieces of legislation adopt a broadly similar approach, requiring a local transport authority or regional transport partnership to:

- set out a proposal
- provide a detailed assessment (a business case)
- get the assessment audited
- consult local operators and other stakeholders
- following the consultation, decide whether to amend the proposal, proceed to implementation or to abort the proposal.

The main difference between England and Scotland is that, north of the border, there is a further stage where permission to proceed must be sought from the Traffic Commissioner. The Commissioner is required to convene an expert panel to consider the proposal, the audit and the consultation results, plus any representations made to them in response to an invitation. After considering these, the expert panel may grant or refuse permission for the proposal to proceed or require amendments to be made.

This is similar to the process adopted in England under the Local Transport Act 2008 but abolished in 2017 following the experience of Tyne & Wear's unsuccessful attempt to introduce a franchise (then known as a "Quality Contract") in 2014 (see paragraph 7.5 below for a further discussion on that case).

Figure M and Figure N illustrate the steps necessary in diagram form. In Scotland, the precise regulations and detailed guidance giving effect to the clauses in the Act were still to be promulgated at the time of writing.

Figure M: Procedures to Introduce Bus Franchising in England

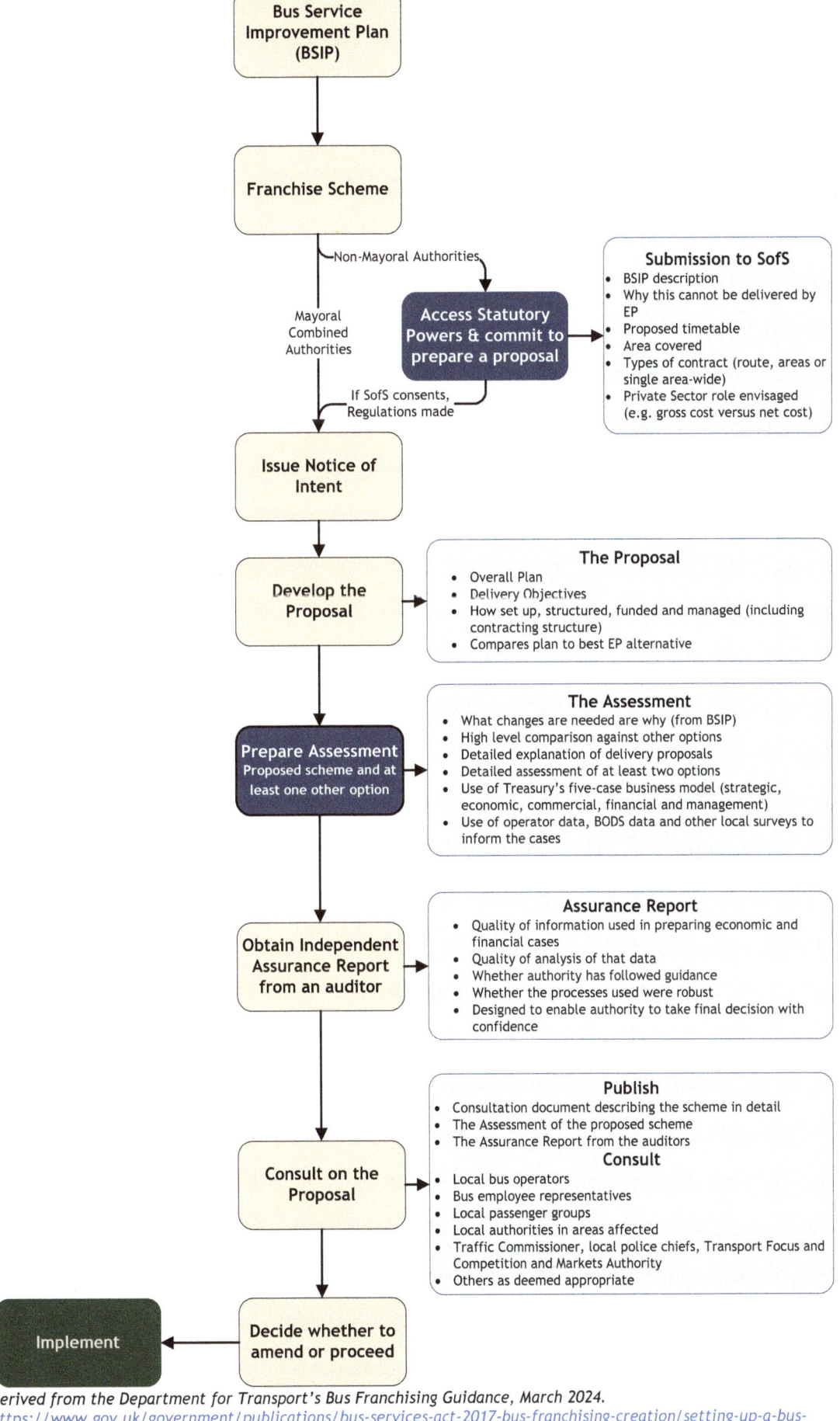

Derived from the Department for Transport's Bus Franchising Guidance, March 2024.
https://www.gov.uk/government/publications/bus-services-act-2017-bus-franchising-creation/setting-up-a-bus-franchising-scheme

In England, the key document in the process is the Bus Service Improvement Plan (BSIP). This sets out the ambition of the local transport authority, the local operators and other stakeholders to improve bus services in their area and the means by which this can be achieved. Any authority seeking to introduce a franchise must demonstrate that their plan is the best way to achieve the improvements in their BSIP.

This is the procedure that the Government is proposing to simplify in its new legislation, the "Better Buses Bill" announced in the King's Speech in July 2024. It is expected that the legislation will focus on two areas, highlighted in dark blue in the diagram at Figure M above.

In the first of these, Access Statutory Powers, the government is expected to abolish the need for non-mayoral authorities to receive the Secretary of State's permission. The Statutory Instrument that, when passed, would give all LTAs the right to implement a franchise if they so wish, subject to the Secretary of State's approval, has been published at the time of writing but is awaiting parliamentary approval.

In the second area, the Assessment, there have been calls from the Local Government Association, the Urban Transport Group and others for the process to be made less onerous – especially in relation to the need to provide a full five-case business case for both the authority's preferred option and for an alternative to the proposal. They argue that this is "going beyond what would be required for a typical capital scheme"[23]. As well as making the requirements less onerous, they suggest that the provision of templates and frameworks to support authorities during the assessment process would help.

In Scotland, the processes illustrated at Figure N are less well-developed, and the chart has been derived from the relevant clauses of the 2019 Act[24]. The detailed regulations and accompanying guidance had yet to be published at the time of writing.

---

[23] *A Smoother Ride: Reviewing the Bus Services Act 2017 to empower local areas. Urban Transport Group and Local Government Association, September 2023.* https://urbantransportgroup.org/system/files/general-docs/UTG%20Report%20-%20A%20Smoother%20Ride%20FINAL_2.pdf
[24] *See* https://www.legislation.gov.uk/asp/2019/17/section/38

Figure N: Procedures to Introduce Local Bus Franchising in Scotland

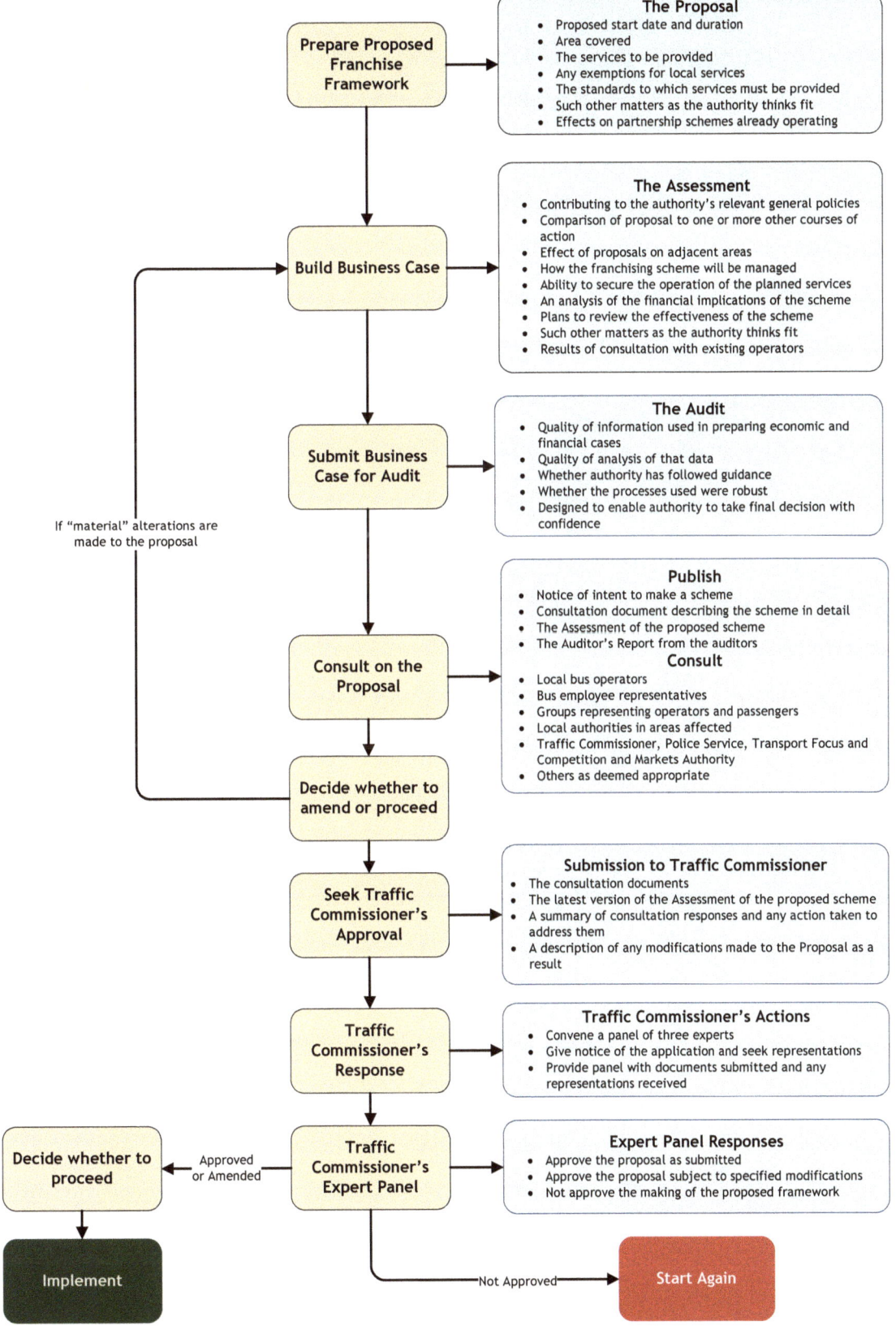

7.5 The Tyne & Wear Experience

One attempt to introduce a Quality Contract Scheme, the precursor to today's bus franchises, was made in England – in Tyne and Wear, where the planned proposals were developed and considered in 2013 and 2014. The scheme proposed by Nexus, the local

Passenger Transport Executive, failed when examined by the QCS Board, an expert panel convened by the Traffic Commissioner[25].

After reviewing over 10,000 pages of written evidence accompanied by 50 hours of oral evidence, the QCS Board published a 70-page report, which stated that, in their view, the QCS failed to meet the requirements of Section 124(i) of the 2000 Transport Act. This was because the proposed scheme:

- could not demonstrate that it would increase use of bus services because its affordability had not been demonstrated
- did not provide value for money
- imposed disproportionate adverse effects on operators.

Additionally, the Board found that Nexus failed to comply with the statutory requirements on consultation specified in section 125 of the Act.

7.6 CMA Guidance

The Competition and Markets Authority (CMA) issued guidance on bus franchising for LTAs in September 2024.[26] As statutory consultees on all franchising proposals, the authority will respond to all future proposals, having already done so in the cases of Greater Manchester, Liverpool City Region, West Yorkshire and Wales.

As well as giving background information on the CMA's role, the 24-page document covers the importance of competition in franchising and the design of franchising. Included in the latter are sections on:

- Access to fleets and depots
- Design of individual franchises
- Transitioning to a franchised network
- Longer term considerations.

---

[25] *Quality Contract Scheme (QCS) Board report on the proposed Tyne and Wear QCS. Accessed via DfT website at: https://www.gov.uk/government/publications/quality-contract-scheme-qcs-board-report-on-the-proposed-tyne-and-wear-qcs*
[26] *https://www.gov.uk/government/publications/bus-franchising-cma-advice-for-local-transport-authorities*

8. Local Authority Ownership

8.1 Historical Context

Municipal ownership has a fundamental part of the public transport scene in the UK since its inception, with many urban tramway schemes coming into local authority ownership during the latter part of the 19th century and early 20th century.

With the progressive abandonment of tramway systems after the First World War, the tramway-owning councils became bus or trolleybus operators instead. Meanwhile, the first licensed municipal motorbus undertaking in Great Britain commenced operation in Eastbourne, East Sussex on 12 April 1903[26].

At the time of the implementation of the 1985 Transport Act, there were 51 council-owned bus undertakings in Great Britain, all of which were converted into wholly owned "arm's length" companies under the requirements of the Act.

Eight remain in local authority ownership, whilst the other 43 no longer exist: six went into administration or were obliged to cease trading whilst 37 were sold by their authorities to other bus companies or management buyout teams. There were four basic reasons for sale:

- Trading performance and/or competition, often resulting from a lack of scale
- Governance issues
- Difficulty raising funds for investment
- A conclusion by the owning authority that scarce capital resources could be employed better elsewhere in the authority or a desire to use the capital receipt elsewhere

In several cases, the demise of the local authority company has occurred in acrimonious circumstances, leaving a difficult legacy for the owning authority, the staff and the public.

8.2 The Current Position

The eight remaining in council hands include five in England, two in Wales and one in Scotland. They are listed in Table 24 below. This gives some demographic data of the companies' home locations (accepting that they may well operate into neighbouring authority areas) and the approximate bus fleet size. It is notable that the surviving companies all operate substantial fleets (the smallest being Ipswich on 80), and all have densely populated urban areas at their heart, with Newport and Warrington having the lowest density.

Enterprise size can be seen as critical, in terms of being able to fund the overheads necessary to support a bus company and meet the obligations that come from being in the public sector. Population density plays a crucial part in determining bus demand in a given area.

It is important to note that local authority ownership does not exempt the companies from fulfilling their statutory and financial obligations, and this includes in many cases the

---

[26] John Hibbs, The History of British Bus Services, David & Charles, 2004

payment of a dividend where possible in order to contribute to the owning councils' other budgetary commitments, as well as the requirements of the Competition Acts.

Table 13: Surviving Municipal Bus Operations in Great Britain

Location	Population (Mid-Year Estimates, 2022)	Area (Km²)	Density (persons per km²)	Fleet Size
Blackpool	141,574	35	4,045	137
Cardiff	372,089	141	2,639	213
Edinburgh	514,990	263	1,958	755
Ipswich	139,247	39	3,570	74
Newport	161,506	191	846	115
Nottingham	328,513	75	4,380	315
Reading	174,820	40	4,371	175
Warrington	211,580	181	1,169	110

8.3 Routes to New Municipal Companies

Given the appropriate legislative powers, there would be two possible routes to council ownership:

- Set up a new wholly owned company to compete with existing operators either by running commercial services or bidding for contracts
- Raise capital to acquire an existing local bus company

Each would require:

- Initial funding to acquire assets
- Working capital
- Funds for future investment
- A business case showing how the business would be viable
- An annual surplus to meet borrowing costs and repay debt (i.e. make a profit)
- The development of appropriate governance structures.

In the current fiscal climate, it would seem unlikely that authorities would have the resources to follow any of these courses, especially in a franchised environment where there would be no guarantee of a contract win.

The survival of existing local authority companies could not be guaranteed in an initial competitive tendering round for a franchise, and, in the same way, the future survival of new local authority owned companies could not be guaranteed in a tendering round.

8.4 The Local Authority Ownership Debate

Strong arguments have been advanced in favour of the retention or return of local authority ownership in bus companies over the years, especially during the passage of new legislation, including the Bus Services Act 2017 in England (which banned the establishment of new companies) and The Transport (Scotland) Act 2019 (which allowed own account operations by local transport authorities).

Campaigning groups have argued strongly against the ban on new local authority bus companies included in the 2017 Act, pointing to the success of operators in Edinburgh, Nottingham and Reading. As the magazine *New Statesman* pointed out in 2018, "a municipal company has won UK Bus Operator of the Year for six of the past ten years", whilst the Urban Transport Group[27] pointed out that two of the companies in England outside London with the highest ridership per head of the population – Nottingham and Reading – were municipally owned.

On the other hand, critics have pointed to the collapse of several companies over the years, most recently Halton Borough Transport, which was declared insolvent in January 2020 in acrimonious circumstances, after severe disagreements between executive and non-executive directors[28]. This was not unique: relationships between the owning council and the bus company's executive directors have not always been smooth over the years, but the Halton case does seem to have been one of the extreme examples.

There can be difficulties, too, in the relationships between council as shareholder and the bus company, and conflicts can arise between Councillors' roles as political representatives and non-executive directors. Such a situation arose in Edinburgh in 2014 and 2015[29]. Such issues need careful management and clear guidelines.

It is expected that the new Better Buses Bill may well lift the ban on new council-owned bus operations, but it remains to be seen how many authorities would seek to use the powers. However, in a world where bus services were mainly or exclusively let by competitive tender, the option of taking operations back in-house could be an important instrument for local transport authorities as an operator of last resort should the contract system break down or was not working satisfactorily.

---

[27] *A Smoother Ride: Reviewing the Bus Services Act 2017 to empower local areas. Urban Transport Group and Local Government Association, September 2023.*
https://www.urbantransportgroup.org/resources/types/report/smoother-ride-reviewing-bus-services-act-2017-empower-local-areas

[28] *Liverpool Echo 4 October 2020, accessed via https://www.liverpoolecho.co.uk/news/liverpool-news/rows-negligence-huge-losses-full-19032457.*

[29] *See* https://www.thenational.scot/news/14897836.management-crisis-at-lothian-buses-goes-on/ *and other local and trade press accounts.*

Part C: The Key Tasks Ahead

Introduction

The pressure on the new Government, local authorities and bus operators to deliver change is immense. The outcomes will affect the new administration's aims across a whole range of economic and social policy, including:

- Economic efficiency, productivity and growth
- Social cohesion, mobility and inclusion
- Housing and land use development
- Health and social care
- Educational, employment and training opportunities
- Environmental issues including local air quality and progress to net zero targets.

Each of these policy areas presents its own unique problems, has undergone its own changes post-Covid and is facing its own challenges in the future. Given the expectations of rapid technological change over the next ten years, the bus industry's watchword needs to be flexibility, enabling it to respond to changing demographics, geography, mobility and journey purpose.

In the short term, the two most pressing challenges are to improve the ***performance*** of existing services and to increase the ***quantum*** of network provision. In this second part of the report, we will focus on the conditions necessary to make progress in these two areas and look to quantify the sums involved in being able to deliver improvements.

In the following chapters, we will go on to consider the requirements for delivering the decarbonisation of the bus industry by the current target date of 2040 – and examine the costs involved.

Regulatory reform is high on the government's list of priorities, with a new Better Buses Bill promised in the King's Speech, designed to simplify and encourage the move to "franchising" in other areas. This will also be affected the new English Devolution Bill, which plans further changes to the local government structure. In areas affected by those plans, further reorganisation may delay any decisions about bus reform. The chapter on regulatory reform considers some of the issues that arise, and also sets them in an international context.

9. Improving Performance

Two issues have dominated the ability of bus operators to deliver reliable services over the last few years – driver recruitment and traffic congestion.

9.1 Driver Recruitment

In the immediate post-pandemic period, competition for qualified drivers across the PSV and HGV industries was intense, and many bus operators throughout the country reported serious shortages of staff, exacerbated by high ongoing infection rates from the various Covid-19 variants, a lack of recruits from the EU following Britain's departure and a significant increase in the number of people unable to work because of long-term health problems. Additionally in the immediate post-lockdown period, there were delays in the processing of applications for both provisional and full PSV licences, whilst social distancing regulations delayed training and testing.

A survey carried out by Confederation of Passenger Transport (CPT), the industry's trade association, in 2022 found a shortage level of 10% (9.3% bus, 15.9% coach). This had eased to 6.5% bus, 12.5% coach during 2023, and stood at 4.5% bus, 9.6% coach in the survey carried out in January 2024. This was the lowest shortage figure since the end of lockdowns in 2021.

A combination of new recruitment campaigns, improved training and wage increases all helped to reduce the shortages, whilst measures to improve staff retention levels have also been taken by many operators around the country.

The phenomenon of staff shortages is by no means new and dates back to the fifties and sixties in parts of the country such as London, Bristol and the West Midlands. Hence London Transport's direct recruitment of staff from the Caribbean in the 1950s, and extensive recruitment by many operators from Eastern Europe after the eastward expansion of the EU in 2004.

Being a bus driver is a demanding job, especially in modern traffic conditions. The job involves working shifts, being on duty at weekends and unsocial hours with long shift lengths. Drivers also need highly developed customer-relations skills, and dealing with the public can be difficult and demanding, especially when there are delays or cancellations. The growth of parcel deliveries associated with online shopping has led to the creation of more than 55,000 additional logistics jobs since 2010[30]. These require similar skills with fewer unsocial hours, similar or higher wage rates and much lower levels of inter-action with the public.

It is therefore important that operators retain the flexibility to adjust wages in different labour markets to enable them to meet recruitment targets, and one of the concerns about franchising proposals is the extent to which that freedom would be removed, especially under gross cost contracts, or by direct attempts by government to influence and constrain wage levels for macro-economic reasons.

The previous Government announced proposed reforms to ease the driver recruitment challenge in the spring of 2024. The consultation period on the reforms closed just before the General Election, so final decisions are awaited.

---

[30] *ONS, Total employment (thousands) by 2, 3 and 5 digit SIC 2007, 2010 compared with 2022. Codes 49410, 53201/2.*

The proposed changes would:

- remove the restriction which prevents bus and coach drivers aged 18 to 20 from driving a regular service greater than 50km in length

- allow a person to undertake the theory and off-road manoeuvres tests required to gain their driver certificate of professional competence (DCPC) before being granted a provisional bus, coach or heavy goods vehicle (HGV) driver entitlement.

- introduce a new category of DCPC for national (as opposed to international) drivers with reduced and more flexible training requirements

9.2 Traffic Congestion and Bus Priority

All the evidence points to a reduction in the average speed of buses since at least the turn of the century, as traffic volumes have grown, and congestion increased.

For example, driver productivity (as measured by kilometres run per driver employed) fell every year from 2005 to 2019, with a difference totalling 9.9%. That meant that 10% more drivers were needed to deliver a given level of service in 2019 than had been the case in 2005.

As we saw in section 2.4 above, improving bus speeds can have a transformational effect on both the cost of operation and the level of passenger demand.

The latest data published by CPT, based on a members' survey[31] showed that bus speeds across Great Britain outside London averaged 12.12 mph (19.36 kph) in February 2024, up from 12.07 mph (19.31 kph) a year earlier. These figures compared with 11.95 mph in the first survey in the series, dated February 2022. In London, much higher congestion levels resulted in an average speed of just 7.6 mph (12.2 kph) in February 2024, though TfL figures suggest higher speeds in outer London boroughs[32].

The question is the extent to which bus priorities on their own can deliver the improvements needed whilst maintaining acceptance by a sceptical public, or whether other measures to restrain demand for travel by private car will be needed. This is particularly important given the need to reach targets set for modal shift in order to deliver net zero targets.

Priority measures can take various forms, including bus lanes, bus gates, bus-only rights of way (busways, guided or not), traffic signal priorities and queue relocation systems – and examples of them all can be found in various locations around the country.

In addition, there are other items which are integral to the provision of a high-quality, well-promoted bus network. These include roadside infrastructure (stops, shelters and information displays, whether static or real time), terminal facilities, bus stations and interchanges.

In a report prepared by KPMG for campaigning group Greener Journeys in 2017, it was estimated that targeted investment in local bus infrastructure and selective priority measures would typically generate £4.90 of net economic benefit for each £1 of cost incurred[33], with further benefits expected in related policy areas such as social welfare and

---

[31] Bus Industry Costs in February 2024, CPT and 2FM Limited, July 2024. https://www.cpt-uk.org/.
[32] For more information, see https://tfl.gov.uk/corporate/publications-and-reports/buses-performance-data#on-this-page-4
[33] 'The True Value of Local Bus Services': A Report to Greener Journeys. KPMG LLP, June 2017. https://www.buscentreofexcellence.org.uk/resources-collection/the-true-value-of-local-bus-services.

public health. This level of return represents high value for money under the Department for Transport's appraisal guidance.

The KPMG report also cites research undertaken by the Institute of Transport Studies at Leeds University for Greener Journeys in 2013 estimated that between 18% and 23% of car users could be encouraged to switch to buses if buses were quicker and more reliable.

Meanwhile, conventional demand elasticities suggest that demand can vary by 0.25% for each 1% change in bus speeds[34]. Thus, a two minute saving on a ten minute journey could result in a 5% increase in patronage, as well as delivering lower operating costs.

---

[34] *The Demand for Public Transport: A Practical Guide, TRL 593. 2004.*
https://trl.co.uk/uploads/trl/documents/TRL593%20-%20The%20Demand%20for%20Public%20Transport.pdf

10. Increasing Service Levels

10.1 Introduction

As we saw in Chapter 1, there have been huge cuts in bus service provision across the whole of Great Britain since 2010. This has partly been driven by falls in demand, but also by cuts in local authority support for "socially necessary" bus services – especially in rural areas (see Table 3 above for more details).

10.2 Reasons for the Increases

There are several reasons why these cuts will need to be reversed in the coming years, including:

- Improving accessibility – providing people with the ability to reach essential services, such as schools, hospitals, GP surgeries and supermarkets, by public transport. Accessibility standards of this sort are essential to underpin a whole range of other government policies in health, education, social care, social mobility and social inclusion

- Providing an alternative to the private car. Achieving modal shift from private car to public transport and active travel modes is a central plank in policies to deliver net zero targets over the next 25 years

- Economic growth: bus service provision is an essential element in promoting economic and productivity growth, including:

    - our ability to provide new housing developments at scale

    - assisting in the revival of town and city centres damaged by retail decline and post-Covid social change

    - providing access to new employment opportunities and other land use developments

    - economic growth: transport efficiency has been shown to be closely linked with improved performance in the economy. Reducing travel time and reducing or eliminating congestion will maximise productive work time and the population's available leisure time. Efficient and attractive bus services will help to achieve this, whilst also improving local air quality and contributing to net zero targets.

Several questions follow from this: firstly, how sustained increases in service levels can be achieved; secondly, who is going to pay; thirdly, whether anybody will use the increased services, and fourthly, how much it will cost.

10.3 Achieving Increases

In the major urban areas, the current likelihood is that the initiative will lie with the combined authorities under a franchise regime. As discussed in Chapter 7, franchising means that the tendering authority specifies all aspects of the network within the franchise area, leaving no room for anybody else to run services. The only exception to this could be on cross-boundary services which might continue to be commercially operated. Were any of the authorities to offer a "net cost" tendering regime (see paragraph 7.3.2 for more details), the winning operator could be empowered to run additional services or extra frequencies at their own risk.

In areas running an Enhanced Partnership regime, the expectation is that service levels and frequencies will form part of the discussion between the partners. In practice, this has been the case for the last four years or more, as operators and authorities became accustomed to work together in the provision of services during the pandemic (indeed, such partnerships were a pre-condition for the payment of Covid revenue support).

10.4 Paying for Services

The clear expectation is that the cost of what might be termed as "development mileage" will have to be met by the public sector. In franchise areas, options would be very limited. Elsewhere, there is little appetite for high levels of risk by commercial operators, and little or no headroom in their financial performance for them to be able to afford it. However, the enhancement of frequencies on already successful commercial services may be undertaken at the operator's risk, but that will depend to an extent on the level of fares charged.

A start was made with the allocation of BSIP Phase 1 money in 2022 (discussed in chapter 4 above), but it is as yet unclear what effect this has had on service levels, since BSIP funding could be spent on new services or frequency enhancements but also on infrastructure and new fares initiatives. BSIP Phase 2 money was primarily concerned with maintaining service levels in the face of continuing failure of demand to recover to pre-Covid levels.

10.5 Patronage Expectations

There is no magic means of measuring the public's response to new or enhanced networks: in busy, densely populated urban areas where bus use is already relatively high, conventional demand elasticities might apply. A number of studies have identified different means of measuring this, based on kilometres run, on passenger waiting times, or on vehicle hours operated[35]. Such measures are also influenced by such factors as urban v rural (elasticities were found to be higher in less densely populated areas) and time of day/day of week (higher when services were less frequent).

Using elasticity measures is very useful in areas or networks where services are well established and statistics for existing demand are available. However, such tools will not exist for areas where services are scheduled for re-introduction, possibly after a gap of several years.

Here, tools such as detailed demographic analysis, trip rate modelling and generalised cost modelling will be useful in estimating potential demand along a given route or corridor.

It is important to establish criteria by which potential demand could justify the introduction of a service, and to decide on parameters by which the success or failure of a service could be judged and over what timescale.

10.6 How Much it Might Cost

10.6.1 Overall Costs

As with demand, much will depend on local circumstances and the results of a tendering exercise, if one is going to be held. In rough terms, as can be seen in Appendix A, we

---

[35] *Discussed in* The Demand for Public Transport: The Effects of Fares, Quality of Service, Income and Car Ownership. *Paulley, N.; Balcombe, R.; Mackett, R.; Titheridge, H.; Preston, J.M.; Wardman, M.R.; Shires, J.D.; White, P. (2006) https://eprints.whiterose.ac.uk/2034/*

estimate that the cost of running a bus in 2024 averages out at approximately £56 per bus hour – that's around £220,000 per year for a single vehicle operation running seven days a week and averaging eleven hours day.

On a larger scale, it is possible to suggest the likely sums that would be required to reach certain service levels, in given areas of the country, and we have constructed a number of scenarios to illustrate this.

10.6.2 Extending the Operating Day

Not all the service improvements available would cost the full £56 an hour to introduce. For example, extending the operating day. The lack of evening and Sunday services has long been a criticism of the deregulated regime outside London, and its effects can clearly be seen in the fact that, on average, buses in London are used for 15½ hours a day, compared with less than 11½ in other parts of the country. London's bus network is characterised by a large number of 24 hour services and an extensive network of special night buses, which inevitably increase the average figure. Utilisation in other urban centres in England is also higher, averaging around 14 hours a day[36].

Extending the operating day would incur additional labour and engineering costs, plus the extra cost of fuel, oil and tyres for the kilometres run – but should not increase overheads or vehicle ownership costs.

We have tested the idea of increasing the existing operating day in each of the principal market sectors by one hour a day, resulting in an increase in hours and kilometres run of around 8.5% across Great Britain outside London. The total cost would be £310m a year, including £50m in Scotland, £16m in Wales and £244m in England outside London. The expected resource requirements are summarised in Table 14 below. Since this option would merely be making more intensive use of the existing fleet, there would be no need for extra vehicles, so there would be no capital expenditure requirement.

Table 14: Resource Implications of Extending the Operating Day by 1 hour

Resource Requirements	English Mets	English Shires	Scotland	Wales	GB Outside London
Additional Km run (million)	32.07	66.89	24.77	7.68	131.41
Operating Costs (£m)	88.7	155.5	49.9	16.0	310.1
Annual Bus Hours (000s)	2,218	3,847	1,157	382	7,604
Extra Drivers	1,417	2,197	744	255	4,613

10.6.3 Restoring Services to Previous Levels

As we saw in paragraph 1.2.2 and Table 3 above, the DfT provides estimates of service levels and patronage in rural and urban areas, based on an ONS categorisation of local authorities (for more details, please see Appendix D).

This enables us to assess separately the likely costs of restoring some or all of the service levels that have been reduced over the years since 2010 in those sub-markets as well as the other geographical sectors.

Because life has changed so much in the intervening years, it is most unlikely that such a restoration would see all the lost services running again. However, the volume of

---

[36] *CPT Cost Monitor.*

kilometres run can give be useful indicator of the resources needed. Clearly, the decisions on future levels will be made locally and circumstances will vary between authorities – but we believe that these figures offer useful "order of magnitude" indications.

The estimates are presented once again by the main market sectors, but this time with the English Shire areas split between the "Other Mainly Urban", "Urban with Significant Rural" and "Largely or Mainly Rural" categories.

Three scenarios have been calculated:

- Restoring kilometres run to 2019 (pre-Covid) levels
- Restoring kilometres run to 2010 levels
- Restoring kilometres run on supported services to 2010 levels.

In each case, the resources required to operate the kilometres have been recalculated using current speeds and vehicle utilisation rates.

10.6.4 Restoring services to 2019 Levels

The results from this scenario are shown in Table 15 below. Depending on the market sector, service levels would need to increase by between 15% and 26% to get the number of kilometres run back to 2018/19 levels. All the mileage concerned was previously operated commercially.

As can be seen, the full cost across the country would be just below £1.6 billion a year, requiring the acquisition of 3,300 extra vehicles at a cost of between £1.2 and £1.5 billion and the recruitment of some 12,700 additional drivers.

Table 15: Restoring Services to 2019 Levels in GB Outside London
Resource Implications by Market Sector

Resource Requirements	English Mets	Other Mainly Urban	Urban with significant rural	Largely or Mainly Rural	England Outside London	Scotland	Wales	Great Britain Outside London
Additional Km run (million)	87	48	52	35	**222**	47	22	**291**
Operating Costs (£m)	508	176	275	254	**1,214**	269	95	**1,578**
Annual Bus Hours (000s)	6,032	785	2,958	2,923	**12,698**	201	1,070	**13,970**
Drivers	3,853	1,813	2,917	2,651	**11,234**	631	826	**12,691**
Vehicles	1,362	186	709	732	**2,989**	48	260	**3,297**
Capex - Lower Range	504	69	262	271	**1,106**	18	96	**1,220**
Capex - Upper Range	640	88	333	344	**1,405**	23	122	**1,549**

10.6.5 Restoring Services to 2010 Levels

Depending on the individual sector, restoration would entail increases in service provision of between 30% and 43%, with an average across Great Britain of 38.22% at an additional annual cost of £2.66 billion. The increase would require the recruitment and training of just over 21,000 drivers and the acquisition of 8,200 additional vehicles at a total cost of between £3.0 and £3.8 billion. The latter requirement might be mitigated to a limited extent by the more efficient use of existing resources.

The resource implications for each market sector are summarised in Table 16 below.

Table 16: Restoring Services to 2010 Levels in GB Outside London
Resource Implications by Market Sector

Resource Requirements	English Mets	Other Mainly Urban	Urban with significant rural	Largely or Mainly Rural	England Outside London	Scotland	Wales	Great Britain Outside London
Additional Km run (million)	172	112	79	87	**450**	102	40	**592**
Operating Costs (£m)	833	521	364	362	**2,081**	429	146	**2,656**
Annual Bus Hours (000s)	11,903	7,226	4,540	4,394	**28,063**	4,783	1,988	**34,835**
Drivers	7,604	4,126	2,593	2,509	**16,831**	3,076	1,330	**21,237**
Vehicles	2,688	1,716	1,088	1,100	**6,592**	1,140	482	**8,214**
Capex - Lower Range	995	635	402	407	**2,439**	422	178	**3,039**
Capex - Upper Range	1,263	807	511	517	**3,098**	536	227	**3,861**

A second option might, at least initially, be the restoration of supported services to 2010 levels. This would meet the NBS strategy and policy aspirations for improving accessibility, especially in rural areas. Using the same methodology and assumptions, the resource implications are summarised in Table 17 below.

As can be seen, the resources required would still be significant, with the increases in supported service kilometrage needing to be more than doubled in three of the market sectors, with an average across Great Britain outside London of 98.8%. The projected annual cost would be £859m, requiring an additional 5,000 drivers and 2,050 vehicles – the latter at a cost of between £1.24 and £1.64 billion. Again, depending on the nature of the services reinstated, there would be some scope to provide services within existing resources. However, given the scale of the cuts imposed since 2010, this may be limited. Not costed here would be the requirement to reopen or provide new depot facilities in some areas.

Table 17: Restoring Supported Services to 2010 Levels

Resource Requirements	English Mets	Other Mainly Urban	Urban with significant rural	Largely or Mainly Rural	England Outside London	Scotland	Wales	Great Britain Outside London
Additional Km run (million)	32	61	54	58	**205**	30	20	**255**
Operating Costs (£m)	122	219	174	169	**685**	108	66	**859**
Annual Bus Hours (000s)	2,213	3,935	3,103	2,929	**12,181**	1,401	994	**14,576**
Drivers	1,413	2,247	1,772	1,673	**3,445**	901	665	**5,011**
Vehicles	500	935	743	734	**1,477**	334	241	**2,052**
Capex - Lower Range	185	346	275	271	**1,077**	124	89	**1,290**
Capex - Upper Range	235	439	349	345	**1,368**	157	113	**1,639**

There are three important points to make about these projections:

- Such restoration could not be done overnight, and in practice could take at least five years to implement

- The figures are not intended as any sort of detailed plan to restore the bus network, but to illustrate the scale of the task that everybody faces if they want to deliver the policy objectives outlined in paragraph 10.2 at the beginning of this chapter.

- As we discussed in paragraph 10.5, decisions to increase service levels would undoubtedly win extra passengers and result in increased revenue, eventually hopefully becoming self-supporting. As we saw, there are several modelling techniques by which the likely response could be estimated, though it is important to understand that additional or returning patronage could typically take months or up to two years to accumulate.

11. Decarbonising the Fleet

11.1 Overview

The industry can point to a good record in emission reduction. According to DfT statistics[37], the industry achieved cuts of 53% in total emissions between 1990 and 2022 (as against a 35.6% fall in mileage[38]), and its 2022 total of 2.8 million tonnes carbon dioxide equivalent (MtCO$_2$e) represented just 0.7% of the UK total, and just 2.2% of 125.7 million emitted by transport as a whole. Travel volumes began to recover from the effects of Covid during the year, as a result of which both mileage and emissions could be expected to grow again as demand recovers.

According to the Department for Energy Security and Net Zero [39], the 2024 figures for greenhouse gas emissions per passenger km for bus were 108.4 grams CO$_{2e}$ per passenger km (g), but this splits out to 74.47g for London and 129.99g for the rest of the country, largely as a result of differing average loads (16.7 for London, 10.1 elsewhere) and the more rapid progress made in the capital to introduce ultra-low and zero emission vehicles. Other public transport modes include 27.17g for coach travel, 35.4g for rail services and 28.6g for light rail.

These figures represent both a problem and an opportunity for the industry: the problem in that there is a potential conflict between running large numbers of empty buses around to fulfil social policy objectives and the need to minimise carbon emissions; the opportunity is to improve occupancy levels, so raising demand for bus travel without increasing carbon emissions.

Although there is not yet a statutory ban on the production and sale of diesel-powered buses and coaches, a proposal was consulted on by the previous government. Meanwhile, the major groups and some other operators have committed themselves to a zero-emission future, typically promising to eliminate their diesel fleets by 2035, ahead of the Government's proposed deadline of 2040. Following the election of a new government, an early decision on the legal position is expected.

Decarbonising the fleet offers a number of challenges, including vehicle costs, infrastructure, electricity supply capacity and the future of government funding assistance.

11.2 Vehicle Costs

These plans are not without a cost, though, since there is a considerable price premium of 25% or more on the purchase of either battery electric or fuel-cell powered vehicles, plus the cost of infrastructure for hydrogen storage or battery charging at depots and – in some cases – at termini.

It is expected that, as the market matures, the price differential for the vehicles will come down – and this is already being affected by price competition. Early interest in the now-defunct Arrival electric vehicle design was strong when it promised no price premium over a diesel vehicle, and the launch in 2024 of a Chinese-built BYD electric double decker priced at £100,000 below the current £500,000 cost of a UK-built vehicle may have been the harbinger of things to come. Another Chinese manufacturer, Yutong, has already

---

[37] *Final UK greenhouse gas emissions national statistics 1990-2021, Department for Transport*
[38] *Road Traffic Statistics Sheet TRA0201. Vehicle Miles for Bus & Coach traffic.*
[39] *2024 Government GHG Conversion Factors for Company Reporting: Methodology Paper for Emission Factors, July 2024*

achieved considerable success in the UK market, and they have also now launched a double deck design. Other European manufacturers such as Volvo, Mercedes and Irizar also offer competition with the UK manufacturers.

Schemes have been developed to enable the retrofitting of battery electric drives to existing diesel vehicles with some success, discussed further in paragraph 11.6 below. The capital cost of repowering is much lower than for a brand new vehicle and will improve the residual value of leased vehicles.

Even if the differential in vehicle prices narrows and repowering proves to be a viable option, the cost of installing electricity supply and connecting it to the grid still has to be met – discussed further below. These costs are unlikely to reduce. Delays that may be experienced in making those connections could well prove to be the main constraint on the market.

11.3 Infrastructure

These costs include:

- the supply of chargers to allow the buses to be connected to mains power
- construction works to install the chargers and make the connection to the grid
- the connection to the grid to get the appropriate levels of electricity into the site, installed by the local Distribution Network Operator (DNO)
- the cost of providing an additional supply if required from the local electricity substation to the bus depot or other site where the charging will be done
- the cost of a new substation and its connection to the grid if there is insufficient capacity at the existing facility.

It follows that the costs vary widely depending on the individual requirements of each site – and this will also the govern the length of time it will take to complete the works.

Evidence to date suggests that the infrastructure cost of electrification is approximately £60,000 per vehicle – though, for the reasons stated, actual numbers will vary quite widely depending on local circumstances.

11.4 Government Funding Assistance

11.4.1 Grant Funding

Government funding has been made available to local transport authorities (LTAs) to assist with the capital cost of introducing zero emission buses outside London, through competitive schemes such as ZEBRA in England and SCOTZEB in Scotland. Funding in Wales has been restricted to services operated on contract to the public sector.

In England and Scotland, the funding has been designed to mitigate the additional unit costs of vehicles – DfT's ZEBRA scheme funded 75% of the difference in cost between the ZEB and a diesel vehicle and contribute to the purchase and installation of the required infrastructure (up to 75% of the cost).

ZEBRA funding

In England, ZEBRA phase one awarded a total of £270 million in two phases, to fund the introduction of 1,278 zero emission vehicles and associated infrastructure across 17 LTA areas in 2021/22 and 2022/23. In March 2023, A further allocation of £25.3 million was awarded to four LTAs to support the introduction of additional zero emission buses for their ZEBRA projects. Phase two of the scheme awarded a further £142.8m of funding, supporting the introduction of a further 955 vehicles across 25 LTAs. This round included £40 million that would be invested in projects that serve predominantly rural areas.

In addition to ZEBRA, the government also awarded funding of £50 million to West Midlands Combined Authority to fund the full electrification of the bus fleet in Coventry by 2025.

ScotZEB Funding

ScotZEB phase one offered awards totalling £62 million to nine bus operators and local authorities for projects involving the introduction of 276 buses and associated charging infrastructure. Phase two, launched in May 2023, offered cash grants towards the cost of vehicles ranging from £60,000 to £135,000 depending on size, and 70% of the infrastructure cost. Applications closed in September 2023, with a further deadline for updated bids in January 2024.

In the event, the winners were announced in July 2024, with a total of just £41.7m awarded to eight operators covering a total of 252 new vehicles and associated infrastructure, including funding for several coach companies as well as local bus operators. In announcing the allocations, Transport Scotland stated that ScotZEB2 would be the final tranche of funding under the ScotZEB approach.

11.4.2 Operating Support

In England, a further incentive is provided by the payment of Bus Service Operators' Grant (BSOG) to operators of zero emission buses at the rate of 22p per kilometre. Because BSOG is still paid on the basis of fossil fuels consumed, operators of electric and fuel cell buses were at a disadvantage. The new payment was introduced in April 2022 on an interim basis pending wider reform of BSOG.

In Scotland, BSOG payments have been made on a per kilometre basis since administration of the grant was devolved in 2010. A low carbon vehicle incentive payment was added, and this has been progressively updated, so that operators of zero emission vehicles currently receive grant at the rate of 30p per kilometre.

11.5 Quantifying the Costs

As already noted in paragraph 3.1.2 above, the average age of the local bus fleet has increased markedly in recent years, thanks to the industry's deteriorating finances and the delays caused by the Covid pandemic. As a result, some 5,850 out of the 34,800 vehicles were more than 15 years old in 2023[40], with a combined replacement cost of around £2.5 billion.

The vast majority of these vehicles are diesel-powered and were built to the more polluting Euro III, Euro IV or Euro V emission standards, which makes their replacement more urgent in terms of local air quality. Altogether, DfT statistics show that in 2023, some 9,800 buses were in service that were built to pre-Euro VI emission standards. We estimate that the replacement cost for this fleet would be £4.4 billion.

---

[40] *Source: PTIS Analysis of Department for Transport Annual Bus Statistics 2023, Sheet BUS06.*

The replacement of the whole local bus fleet with zero emission vehicles by 2035 is likely to require capital expenditure of approximately £13.7 billion - £9.8 billion for Great Britain outside London and a further £3.8 billion for London. The figures are summarised in Table 18 below.

Table 18: Fleet Replacement Needs, 2023

Item	London	English Mets	English Shires	Scotland	Wales	GB Outside London
Fleet Size (000s)	8.79	7.73	13.63	3.22	1.45	26.03
Average Age (Years)	9.2	11.3	11.7	9.0	11.1	11.2
No of Pre-Euro VI vehicles	92	2,032	6,717	589	813	10,151
Weighted ZEB unit cost (£000) †	491	471	430	464	387	
New ZEBs needed by 2035 (000s)	7.83	6.55	11.91	2.41	1.27	22.14
Total Capex Estimate (£m)	3,844	3,084	5,122	1,116	492	9,815

Fleet size and age profile from Department for Transport Annual Bus Statistics 2023.
† - Weighted by fleet profile, reflecting the estimated replacement cost of different vehicle types in the fleet.

More detailed analysis is shown in Table 19 below. This shows the number of vehicles in each market segment that were at or beyond a 15 year life in 2023, and the number that will reach this age in each subsequent year up to 2035. This highlights the investment backlog that has built up in the markets outside London. The figures assume maintenance of current fleet sizes (i.e. without shrinkage in response to further patronage declines or increases in response to modal switch), and the maintenance of current unit prices for new vehicles.

Table 19: Fleet Replacement Requirements by Year
Based on a 15 year life

Year to 31 March	London	English Mets	English Shires	Scotland	Wales	GB Outside London
2024	200	1,509	3,399	438	302	5,648
2025	496	391	665	84	58	1,198
2026	890	420	842	137	60	1,459
2027	705	609	936	232	99	1,876
2028	543	653	956	222	158	1,989
2029	668	566	921	190	134	1,811
2030	704	599	926	272	195	1,992
2031	1,122	523	893	153	92	1,661
2032	975	351	776	155	89	1,371
2033	737	272	638	222	43	1,176
2034	457	341	559	221	21	1,143
2035	332	315	403	79	21	818

11.6 Repowering

The costs and volumes of new EVs required can be mitigated by a programme of retrofitting of existing diesel vehicles with new electric drive trains. The Energy Saving Trust has developed the zero emission vehicle repower accreditation scheme (ZEVRAS), which aims to help the transition to zero emission buses and coaches in the UK. Approved vehicles qualify for the additional BSOG payments and enter clean air zones free of any charge.

Several firms have entered the market – including engineering firm Equipmake, bus manufacturer Wright Bus, who in the Spring of 2024 opened a facility specifically for this purpose at the former Arrival plant in Bicester, Oxfordshire. Zenobē expanded into retrofitting from its position as supplier and installer of electrification equipment at depots. The company has pioneered Electric Transport as a Service (ETaaS), in which vehicles, battery replacement, charging and grid infrastructure, depot-based second-life battery systems, smart charging software, spare parts, and full operational support are all provided to the operator for a single monthly fee.

Zenobē advises[41] that vehicles selected for conversion need to be capable of delivering at least five more years of service, arguing that otherwise the conversion costs will be too high to be recovered over the remaining life of the vehicle. It does not make sense to retrofit an end-of-life diesel or diesel-electric hybrid, as the cost to do so will be high relative to the remaining useful life of the vehicle.

Overall, the company says, repowering is best suited to vehicles with lower mileages and lighter use. That includes tour buses, school buses, or regional buses. An 'easy life' for vehicles is key, since an existing vehicle will not necessarily be able to accommodate as many battery units as a new one, and therefore lower daily mileages or opportunity charging at termini would be needed.

The figures quoted[42] for repowering suggest a cost of around £200,000 per vehicle, which represents a major saving over the cost of a brand new vehicle, with a conversion time of three to four weeks.

The suggestions made by Zenobē for the type of vehicle most suitable for repowering would appear to rule out the majority of vehicles currently operating in London and the English Metropolitan areas, but include the majority in the English Shires, Scotland and Wales. Some routes in outer London might be suitable (we've assumed 5%); similarly, those in outlying areas of the conurbations (we've assumed 10%). At the same time, there would be areas around the big cities in the Shires, which might not be suitable leaving a total of 80% there, with Scotland at 60% and Wales at 90%. Looking at the age criterion, the number of vehicles that were nine years old or younger (excluding London and the English Mets) was around 9,800 in 2023.

The details of our analysis are contained in Table 20 below, alongside our assessment of the potential. The total number of units involved outside the capital would be around 5,700, with a market potential of £1.13 billion. The cost saving compared with the purchase of brand new vehicles would be of the order of £1.32 billion. In London, the limited potential we estimate at 245 units, costing £49m, but saving just under £18m. In

---

[41] Article by Bradley Fox, Business Development Manager at Zenobē, Route One magazine, 24 June 2024. https://www.route-one.net/
[42] See Wrightbus website at https://www.electrive.com/2024/06/21/wrightbus-launches-re-powering-service-for-electric-buses/

all cases, the cost of providing the infrastructure would remain unchanged, and indeed might increase if there were a need for additional opportunity charging equipment.

Table 20: Estimation of Market Potential for Repowering

Item	London	English Mets	English Shires	Scotland	Wales	GB outside London
Buses <=10 years old †	4,900	2,706	4,797	1,765	571	9,839
% eligible for repower	5.0%	10.0%	80.0%	60.0%	90.0%	57.7%
No. eligible for repower	245	271	3,837	1,059	514	5,681
Cost of repowering ‡	48,996	54,125	767,450	211,802	102,855	1,136,231
Cost of new (£000)	66,781	116,342	1,649,633	491,486	198,934	2,456,395
Saving (£000)	17,785	62,217	882,183	279,684	96,080	1,320,163

† *Fleet age details from PTIS analysis of Department for Transport Annual Bus Statistics 2023, Sheet BUS06*
‡ *Costed at £200k per vehicle*

12. Net Zero and Modal Shift

12.1 The Historic Context

The growth of mass car ownership from the 1950s powered a revolution in the demand for travel, and this has been measured over the years by the DfT in its annual Transport Statistics Great Britain publication. This can be traced in Figure O, showing demand has gone up by leaps and bounds over the years, though growth was stalled by fuel crises and economic downturns every few years, until the Covid pandemic slammed everything into reverse.

Figure O: Demand for Travel by Mode, 1952-2022, Great Britain

Source: Transport Statistics Great Britain 2023, Department for Transport, Sheet TSGB0101

As the graph shows, bus and coach services enjoyed a dominant position in the market for travel, with 42% of total demand in 1952. This compared with 18% for rail systems, 27% for cars, vans and taxis, 11% for pedal cycles and 3% for motorcycles. Then came the impact of television ownership and the spread of private car ownership during the 1950s. Thus, by 1960, as the first motorways were opening, and car production was fully into its stride, bus and coach's market share had fallen to 28%. Passenger kilometres travelled by car had doubled in eight years and stood at 139 billion: this accounted for 49% of the 282 billion total for that year.

In 1974, the rise in oil prices and the economic problems brought about by double-digit inflation prompted the first pause in the growth of demand for car travel since 1952. By this time though, the number of passenger kilometres travelled by car had more than doubled again. It stood at 333 billion, accounting for 76% of the total, which had now reached 441 billion. Meanwhile, the share for buses and coaches had dwindled to only 14%.

By the time Iraqi invaded Kuwait in 1990, triggering another spike in oil prices, the bus industry's market share had halved again to 7%. Meanwhile, the private car had achieved a market share of 85%. At the same time, total demand had reached 690 billion. This meant that the total distance travelled by car had increased by a factor of ten since 1952 and stood at 588 billion kilometres.

After a pause at the end of the 1990s, car demand resumed its upward path, reaching a new record of 674 billion kilometres in 2007. Thereafter, the onset of the recession and other social changes drove the number back down. It fell back to a low point of 641 billion in 2013 before beginning to recover as the economy picked up once more, and petrol prices began to fall. The figure peaked in 2019 at 699 billion before the onset of Covid. Bus and coach enjoyed a market share of 3.9% during that year, before dropping to just 2.5% during the pandemic, but recovering to 3.3% in 2022.

12.2   The First Targets

From the mid-1960s onwards, campaigners began to express concern about the sustainability of our lifestyles and the effects of pollution and carbon emissions on the planet. In order to address these concerns, the then Prime Minister Harold Wilson announced the establishment of a standing Royal Commission on Environmental Pollution (RCEP) in December 1969. RCEP took office during 1970 and published its first report the following year.

In 1992, the Commission turned its attention to transport, producing is conclusions in its 18th report, *Transport and the Environment*[43] published in October 1994. The 322-page report noted that in 1992, 12% of passenger kilometres were travelled by public transport, with 21% in Denmark and Italy, 18% in France and 16% in Germany. The report made a total of 110 recommendations, including that the proportion of passenger kilometres travelled by public transport should rise from the 12% calculated for 1991 to 20% by 2005 30% by 2020. This was to be achieved by a wide range of measures including a doubling of fuel duty in real terms by 2005, extensive bus priority measures and enhanced investment in rail. In our *Bus Industry Monitor* publication at the time, we pointed out the scale of change that would be required in order to deliver such a shift, with each 1% of car demand moved to public transport requiring increases of 13.7% in bus demand or 15.8% on the rail network.

12.3   The Blair Government's Response

The RCEP's recommendations, updated in its 20th report in 1997, were a powerful driver behind the Blair government's move to increase public transport investment and drive change, passing the Transport Act 2000 and publishing a 10-year plan for investment. The economic case for continuing this was made by the 2005 Eddington Report, which noted the importance of an efficient transport system to future economic growth.

For a while, the proposition seemed to be working. Powered by overall economic growth, demand for travel by all modes had grown by over 13% by the time Labour left office in 2010, compared with the RCEP's 1992 base. Car passenger kilometres had grown by a smaller percentage, 10.5%, whilst public transport demand had grown by over 36% - thanks to a 68% surge in rail demand and a 5.2% increase in passenger kilometres travelled by bus. Car travel's market share had fallen from 85.4% in 1992 (and an even higher 86.3% in 1997) to 83.5% in 2010.

---

[43] *A copy is available for purchase via the National Archives. The document has not been digitised and cannot be read online or downloaded. Also published by the Oxford University Press, ISBN 0-19-826065-2*

The government passed new legislation in the form of the Climate Change Act 2008, which amongst other things, set a target of 2050 for an 80% reduction in UK emissions of targeted greenhouse gases, established a system of five-yearly "carbon budgets" and established the new Committee on Climate Change.

12.4 A Change of Emphasis

Though on the surface, the new coalition government remained committed to green targets set by its predecessors, but there was a change of emphasis – including an end to what several Conservative politicians had called "the war on the motorist". In his 2011 budget, the Chancellor George Osborne cancelled a planned 4% inflation-related increase in fuel duty and indeed reduced the charge by 1p per litre. It has remained frozen at this level ever since, being given a "temporary" 5p cut for 2022/23, subsequently extended until 2024/25. As part of the austerity programme, the RCEP was abolished in 2011.

At the same time, the government announced that it would reduce the Bus Service Operators' Grant in England by 20% from April 2012. Meanwhile, cuts imposed on local government spending began to affect the level of supported services across the country, as was noted in Chapter 1. By 2019, passenger km travelled by bus had fallen by more than 12 billion or 26% since 2010.

A series of crises over funding and other issues began to hit the rail industry, with major investment projects postponed or cancelled in an attempt to control costs and cuts imposed on Network Rail's maintenance budgets designed to drive efficiency savings. Despite this, rail demand continued to grow until the pandemic, by which time it was 24% above 2010 levels.

Overall, public transport's market share had fallen back to 13.6% from the 2010 level of 14.2%. By 2022, after the impact of Covid, this had fallen back to 11.9%, only slightly ahead of where it had been back in 1992. The principal changes discussed here are summarised in Table 21 below.

The market share enjoyed by buses and coaches was remarkably stable from the early 1990s onwards, maintaining a level of around 6%. However, a 2005 update to the methodology for estimating bus and coach demand revised the figures downwards, and it stood at around five per cent for several years, before dropping again from 2010 onwards. The last pre-Covid figure was 3.9%, dropping to just 2.5% during the pandemic before recovering to 3.3% in 2022. Figure P below tracks the evolution of the market share between 1992 and 2022.

Table 21: Demand for Travel by Mode in GB – Summary Table

Calendar Year	Bus & Coach	Cars, Vans & Taxis	Rail	Air (Domestic)	Other	Total Demand	Total PT
Passenger Km (billions)							
1952	92.0	58.0	38.0	0.2	29.9	218	130.0
1992	42.5	583.0	38.3	4.8	14.0	683	80.8
1997	43.2	632.4	42.2	6.8	8.4	733	85.4
2010	44.7	644.3	64.7	7.8	9.8	771	109.4
2019	32.6	697.8	80.4	9.2	10.6	831	113.1
2022	24.2	636.8	64.0	4.3	10.9	740	88.2
% Split							
1952	42.2%	26.6%	17.4%	0.1%	13.7%	100.0%	59.6%
1992	6.2%	85.4%	5.6%	0.7%	2.1%	100.0%	11.8%
1997	5.9%	86.3%	5.8%	0.9%	1.1%	100.0%	11.7%
2010	5.8%	83.5%	8.4%	1.0%	1.3%	100.0%	14.2%
2019	3.9%	84.0%	9.7%	1.1%	1.3%	100.0%	13.6%
2022	3.3%	86.0%	8.7%	0.6%	1.5%	100.0%	11.9%
% change							
1952-1992	(53.8%)	905.2%	0.8%	2300.0%	(53.1%)	213.0%	(37.8%)
1992-2010	5.2%	10.5%	68.9%	62.1%	(30.4%)	13.0%	35.4%
1997-2010	3.5%	1.9%	53.3%	15.0%	16.7%	5.2%	28.1%
2010-2019	(27.0%)	8.3%	24.3%	18.2%	8.9%	7.7%	3.3%
2019-2022	(25.8%)	(8.7%)	(20.4%)	(53.0%)	2.6%	(10.9%)	(22.0%)

Figure P: Bus & Coach Market Share of Travel Demand since 1992

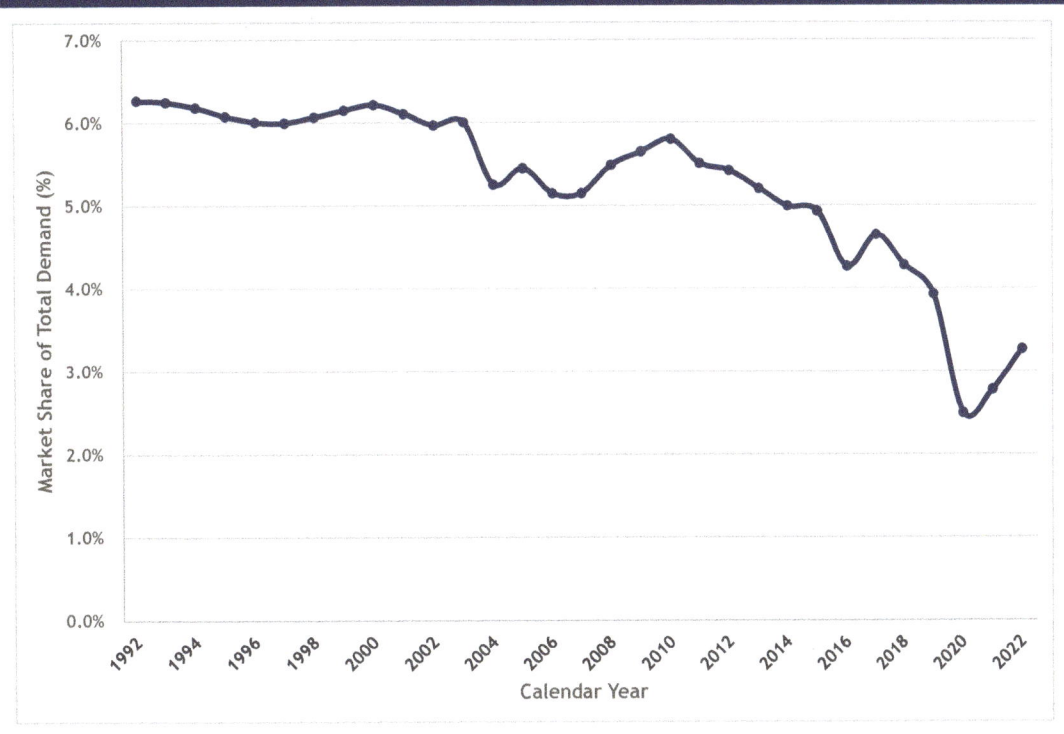

12.5 The Current Targets

The Fifth Carbon Budget, drawn up by the Committee on Climate Change (CCC), was given statutory effect in 2016, and covers the years 2028 to 2032. The budget includes a four megaton reduction in CO_2 ($MtCO_2$) to be achieved by shifting 5 per cent of car km taken in trips of the shortest length (<4 miles for bus, <2 miles for cycling and <1 mile for walking) to bus, cycling and walking. In drawing up the budget, the committee further suggested that reducing car distance travelled by 10% could lower emissions by 6 $MtCO_2$ by 2030.

The sixth Carbon Budget[44], published in December 2020, identified a "balanced net zero pathway for surface transport", delivered by a take-up of zero-emission technologies and reduction in travel demand. These could combine to reduce surface transport emissions by around 70% to 32 $MtCO_{2e}$ by 2035 and to approximately 1 $MtCO_{2e}$ by 2050. As part of this pathway, the committee advised that, compared with baseline growth, approximately 9% of car miles could be reduced (e.g. through increased homeworking) or shifted to lower-carbon modes (such as walking, cycling and public transport) by 2035, increasing to 17% by 2050.

12.6 Transport Decarbonisation Plan

There was concern amongst CCC members and lobby groups that DfT policies were not fully aligned with such a target, with little or no indication of any measures to deliver modal shift in their approach, which has been focused solely on decarbonisation of the vehicle fleet. In October 2018, CCC Chair Lord Debden wrote to then Transport Secretary Chris Grayling, expressing concern that DfT policies had not been adapted to contribute to the need to reduce car travel. Meanwhile, the Department's National Road Traffic Forecast in 2018 suggested road traffic increases of between 17% and 51% between 2015 and 2050 - with consequential growth in traffic congestion.

In response, the Department for Transport promised the development of a detailed Transport Decarbonisation Plan, scheduled to be finalised by the autumn of 2020, and to this end published a consultation document, *Decarbonising Transport – Setting the Challenge*, in March 2020, just as the coronavirus crisis was taking hold.

One of the six strands set out in the document concerns "accelerating modal shift to public and active transport". Under that, four objectives were set:

- Help make public transport and active travel the natural first choice for daily activities
- Support fewer car trips through a coherent, convenient and cost-effective public transport network; and explore how we might use cars differently in future
- Encourage cycling and walking for short journeys
- Explore how to best support the behaviour change required.

The Department emphasised that modal shift was one of its priorities:

> "Accelerating modal shift to public and active transport:
>
> We want public transport and active travel to be the natural first choice for our daily activities. An important aspect of reducing emissions from transport will be

---

[44] https://www.theccc.org.uk/publicationtype/report/carbon-budget/

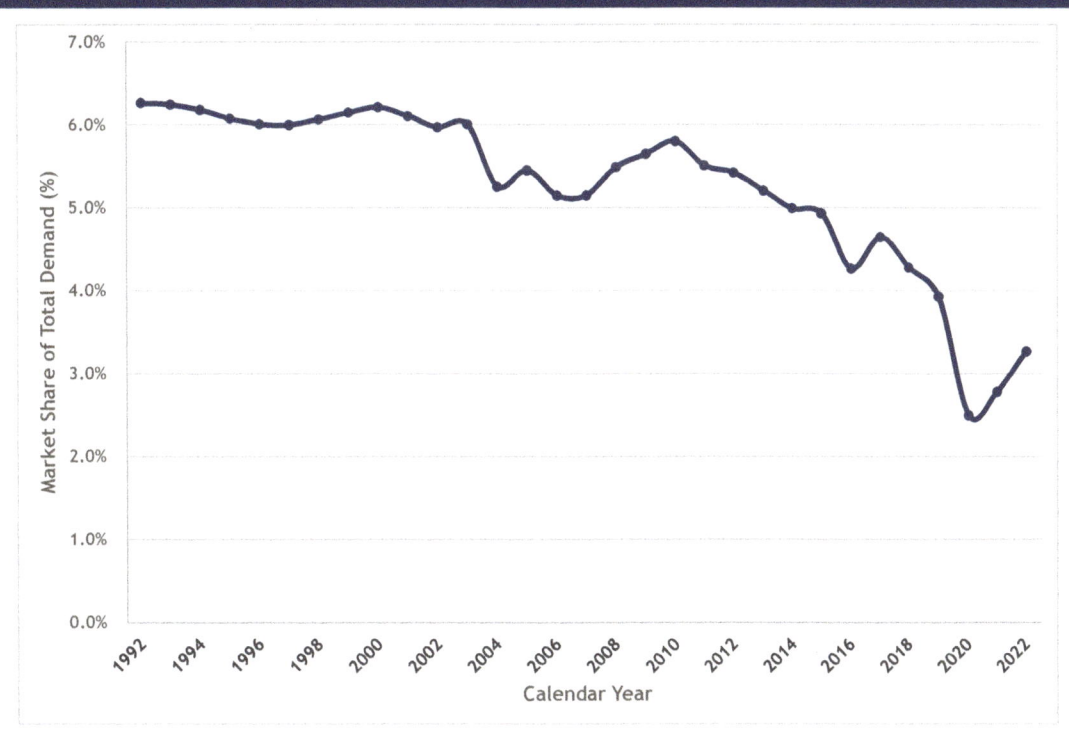

to use our cars less and be able to rely on a convenient, cost-effective and coherent public transport network. For those able to do so, we would like cycling and walking to be the easy and obvious choice for short journeys. We are already exploring how we can use vehicles differently, such as through shared mobility. New technologies and business models may help facilitate modal shift, such as Mobility as a Service platforms. This will require behavioural changes, and we will consider how government and others can support this shift through infrastructure and encouraging those forms of travel."

The plan itself, *Decarbonising Transport: a Better, Greener Britain*, was published in July 2021[45]. Writing in its introduction, the then Transport Secretary Grant Shapps said that the government aimed to reduce urban road traffic overall. "Improvements to public transport, walking and cycling, promoting ridesharing and higher car occupancy, and the changes in commuting, shopping and business travel accelerated by the pandemic, also offer the opportunity for a reduction or at least a stabilisation, in traffic more widely."

Despite this, the Department also published a new set of National Road Traffic Projections[46] in 2022. These envisaged traffic growth of between 8% and 54% between 2025 and 2060, with a core scenario envisaging a 22% increase. Congestion (measured in delay per mile) was also projected to increase, with the average delay per mile projected to increase around 27% between 2025 and 2060. Reconciling the decarbonisation plan with projections based largely on economic and demographic factors is likely to prove very challenging.

12.7   What the Targets Might Mean

The shifts identified as necessary in the fifth and sixth Climate Change Budgets are measured in percentage changes in the distance travelled by private car. Thus, in order to quantify what is involved, we need to refer to the total distance travelled by private car and relate that to the number of passenger kilometres travelled (which is higher because there is more than one person in a car on many journeys).

In the CCC's base year of 2019, the total distanced travelled by private cars, vans and taxis in Great Britain was 509.2 billion kilometres[47]. Passenger kilometres travelled by car, van and taxi in that year are estimated at 697.8 billion[48], giving an average vehicle occupancy of 1.37.

Reducing the number of passenger km travelled by car, van and taxi by 1% would cut demand by 7.0 billion passenger kilometres. As the CCC suggests, this would involve some reduction of overall travel demand (home working or more online shopping, for example) but also a switch of journeys to other modes, such as cycling, walking or public transport.

In that same year, the total travelled by bus and coach was 32.6 billion passenger km, 3.9% of the total. If all seven billion were to switch from car to bus and coach, it would represent an increase from 32.6 billion to 39.6 billion, or 28.8%. At current average

---
[45] See https://assets.publishing.service.gov.uk/media/610d63ffe90e0706d92fa282/decarbonising-transport-a-better-greener-britain.pdf
[46] See https://www.gov.uk/government/publications/national-road-traffic-projections
[47] Road Traffic Estimates, Department for Transport, Sheet TRA0201.
[48] Transport Statistics Great Britain, Sheet TSGB0101a.

journey lengths, 5.92 km (3.68 miles)[49], the 7.0 billion passenger km equates to 1.18 billion passenger journeys, or 31.5% of the current levels.

In practice, the picture is much more complex. Journeys vary in length, duration and purpose, each of which will affect people's propensity to switch to a different mode. Data from the National Travel Survey provides a breakdown of current journey-making by distance, which we can translate into estimates of passenger kilometres. The analysis is illustrated in the graphs at Figure Q and Figure R below.

These two charts illustrate the wide variations between the two measures: trips of less than one mile account for more than a quarter of total demand for journeys, but the short distance covered by each trip means that they only account for just over 2% of passenger kilometres. At the other end of the scale, trips of 100 miles or more account for just 0.6% of the total, and yet account for almost 18% of passenger kilometres travelled.

Using the detail contained in NTS9916 and applying the results to the picture for national demand provided by Transport Statistics Great Britain (TSGB0101), we provide some estimates of what might happen at given levels of modal switch away from car.

Figure Q: Passenger Journeys by Distance Travelled, England, 2022

- 25 to <50: 2.8%
- 50 to <100: 1.1%
- 100+: 0.6%
- 10 to <25: 10.4%
- < 1 Mile: 25.9%
- 5 to <10: 13.7%
- 1 to <2: 20.2%
- 2 to <5: 25.2%

Source: National Travel Survey 2022, Department for Transport, Sheet NTS9916

---

[49] *PTIS Analysis of Annual Bus Statistics, Department for Transport, Sheets BUS01 and BUS03*

Figure R: Estimated Passenger Km by Distance Travelled, England, 2022

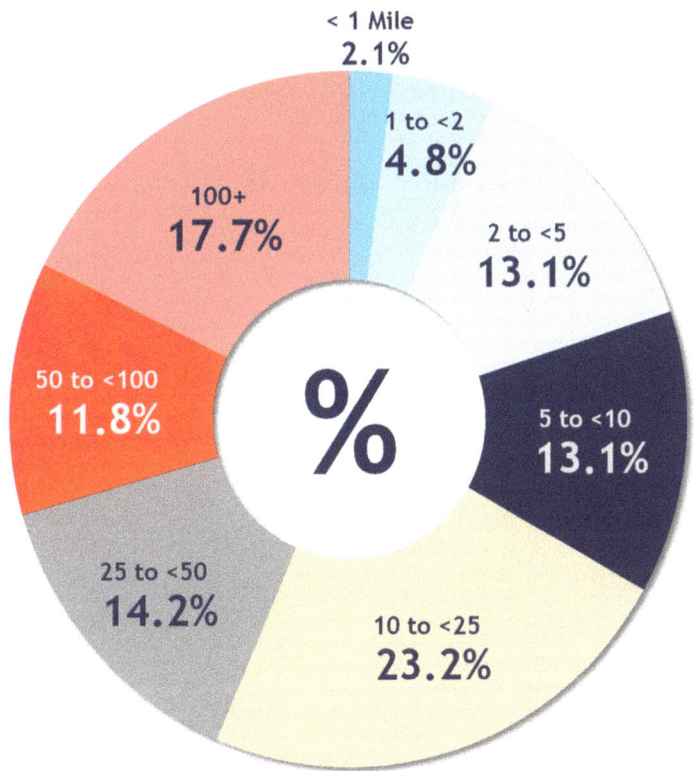

Source: PTIS Estimates of average journey length, based on NTS9916, with passenger km reconciled to totals per person per year in NTS0101.

The results of this for the bus industry are summarised in Table 22 below. As with all modelling of this nature, the estimates require assumptions to be made which may or may not prove to be correct:

- Firstly, that a given percentage reduction in car use would be spread equally amongst all journey distances
- Secondly, that the mode to which the journey is switched would be selected in line with current market proportions.

Table 22: Estimated Bus Demand Gains from Modal Switch

Item	< 1 Mile	1 to <2	2 to <5	5 to <10	10 to <25	25 to <50	50 to <100	100+	All lengths	% change
Passenger KM Switched to bus (millions)										
5% switch	1	75	1,824	2,039	1,511	291	248	260	6,249	25.8%
9% switch	2	135	3,283	3,671	2,719	523	446	468	11,248	46.5%
17% switch	3	256	6,202	6,934	5,136	988	843	885	21,247	87.8%
Passenger Journeys Implied (millions)										
5% switch	1	31	349	211	67	6	2	1	668	17.8%
9% switch	2	56	628	380	121	10	4	2	1,203	32.1%
17% switch	4	106	1,186	718	228	19	8	3	2,272	60.7%

These estimates show a more nuanced picture of the potential for modal shift specifically to bus and coach. The numbers of journeys involved are still substantial, but relating the possible gains to current levels of demand points to short-term market recovery rather than spectacular gains: thus:

- A 5% switch from current levels would result in growth of 668 million passengers from 2022/23 levels, taking the total to 4.41 billion, still well short of the pre-Covid total in 2018/19 of 4.79 billion.

- Under the 9% scenario, growth of 1.2 billion would take patronage to 4.95 billion, a total last seen as recently as 2017/18

- A 17% reduction in car use could really make a big difference, taking bus patronage to just over 6 billion, a figure last seen in the early 1980s.

Given that travel demand was still recovering from the effects of Covid in 2022/23, it may be that using that year as a base is setting the bar too low, but that can only be judged when later figures are published.

12.8 Modal Shift Targets in Scotland

In its 2023 progress report, Progress in Reducing Emissions in Scotland[50], published in March 2024, the CCC expressed concern about the deliverability of one of the Scottish Government's key Net Zero targets, saying:

> "A clear strategy is urgently needed on how the 20% car-km reduction by 2030 target will be achieved and 20-minute neighbourhoods will be implemented. The Scottish Government should provide clear timelines of when these will be published and how the 2030 car-km target will be met."

This was one of many concerns expressed in the report, which led the Scottish Government to scrap its ambitious targets, replacing them by a five-yearly programme of Climate Change Budgets similar to those used by the UK and Welsh Governments.

As with the figures for Great Britain as a whole, it is important to understand the size of the change needed to meet the target, which was set at reducing private car mileage by 20% by 2030. Table 23 below presents the 2022/23 picture of travel demand by mode, from which it can be seen that motoring dominates the picture, accounting for almost 96% of total demand.

Table 23: Travel Demand and Mode Share in Scotland, 2022/23

Mode	Passenger Kilometres (Millions)	Mode Share
Car, Van and Taxi†	67,872.6	93.0%
Bus	2,102.0	2.9%
Rail ‡	2,317.5	3.2%
Motorcycles	272.0	0.4%
Cycling	422.0	0.6%
Total Demand	72,986.1	100.0%

† Calculated traffic estimate of 43.7 bn km @ 1.55 persons per vehicle.
‡ - Rail demand includes Glasgow Subway and Edinburgh tram
Source: 2FM Analysis of figures from Stats Wales, DfT and ORR.

---

[50] https://www.thecc.org.uk/publication/progress-in-reducing-emissions-in-scotland-2023-report-to-parliament/?chapter=chapter-2-sector-progress#2-1-transport

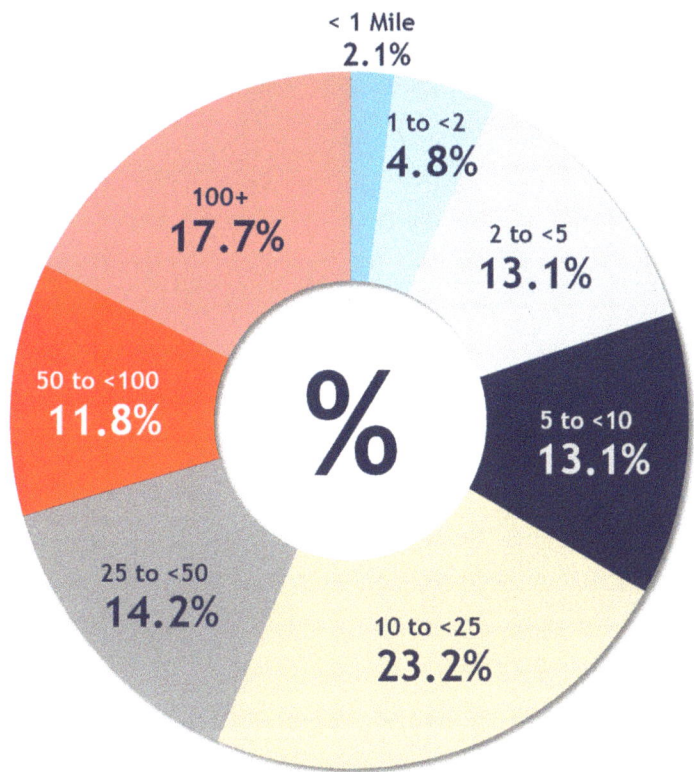

Thus, the achievement of a 20% reduction would see a fall in car mileage of nine billion. Given that vehicle occupancy rates remained unchanged, this would equate to a fall of 13.4 billion passenger kilometres. Each 1% of reduction would equate to a 26% increase in bus demand or a 29% boost to rail travel.

An additional complication is that 45.8% of road traffic is on rural roads, where alternatives to car travel are more difficult and expensive to deliver. Motorway traffic accounts for another 17.5% of road use, mainly on inter-urban journeys. This leaves 37% of traffic moving in urban areas. Thus, it could be expected that the burden of traffic reduction would fall most heavily on urban areas, where measures such as parking policy, park and ride and even congestion charging can be used to deliver modal shift.

12.9 Modal Shift Targets in Wales

In its 2023 Progress Report *Reducing Emissions in Wales*[51] published in June 2023, the CCC set eight specific targets for the Welsh Government towards the achievement of the Climate Change Budgets currently in force. One target was associated with transport, namely to:

> "Develop and publish a full delivery plan for how to realise the ambition of reducing per-person car demand by 10% by 2030. This should include consideration of how measures that limit car usage will interact with those that enable more sustainable modes."

Again, it is important to understand the size of the change involved. Table 24 below shows the levels of transport demand in Wales in 2022/23, from which it will be seen that travel by car, van and taxi is estimated to account for 95.9% of total demand in Wales, totalling some 44 billion passenger kilometres. Reducing that figure by 10% by 2030 would mean a reduction of 4.4 billion passenger km, taking traffic back to levels last seen a decade ago.

As with previous CCC reports, it is envisaged that the target would be achieved by a combination of travelling less (e.g. working and/or shopping from home) and mode shift to active travel and public transport.

Looking at figures for mode share in Wales in Table 24, we see that cars, vans and taxis currently account for over 96% of existing demand.

Table 24: Travel Demand and Mode Share in Wales, 2022/23

Mode	Passenger Kilometres (Millions)	Mode Share
Car, Van and Taxi†	44,102.4	95.9%
Bus	487.4	1.1%
Rail	989.1	2.2%
Motorcycles	200.0	0.4%
Cycling	190.0	0.4%
Total Demand	45,968.9	100.0%

† Calculated as from kilometres DfT traffic estimate of 29.9 bn km @ 1.55 persons per vehicle.
Source: 2FM Analysis of figures from Stats Wales, DfT and ORR.

---

[51] https://www.theccc.org.uk/publication/2023-progress-report-reducing-emissions-in-wales/#recommendations-to-government

Meanwhile, bus and rail travel continued to struggle to recover to pre-pandemic levels. As a result, quite small shifts to either public transport mode would represent a huge increase in demand. Each one per cent of car demand that switched to bus would represent a 50% increase from 2022/23 levels. A similar number switching to rail would increase demand by 48%.

As in Scotland, the distribution of traffic by road type will have a significant effect on how traffic reduction targets can be achieved. Analysis shows that 57.9% of Welsh traffic is on rural roads, with another 12.4% on the motorway network. This leaves 29.8% on urban roads, where a wider range of policies is available to encourage modal shift.

Appendix A: Sustainable Profits - A Worked Example

1. Introduction

To provide an illustration of this methodology in action, we have reconstructed the finances of three notional bus companies. We have done this with the assistance of data from our *Bus Industry Monitor* database, together with expert advice from within the industry.

Each company has 200 buses running from three depots in the English Shires, a PTE area and in London. In each case, the fleets comprise a mixture of smaller and larger buses including double deckers. Outside London, the fleets have an average age of eight years, in line with the Government's targets; in London, the average age is lower at around 4 years.

We have calculated:

- the value of the fleet based on its age distribution and historic capital costs
- the value of land and buildings required for head office and depot functions
- the value of fixtures, fittings, plant and equipment required
- the value of other balance sheet elements, such as current assets (debtors, stocks and cash) and current liabilities (creditors), based on expected proportions of trading volumes
- how the assets of the business are likely to have been financed, using a mixture of shares (equity) and borrowing from banks or other providers (debt). In practice this varies between businesses on the ground, often for purely historical reasons.

In the case of the London operation, we have assumed that around 60% of the fleet is held on operating leases; this means that the buses concerned do not appear on the balance sheet, and the lease rental payments are included in operating costs (see paragraph 11. for a further discussion of this issue).

The analysis is designed illustrate the levels of operating profit required by operators in different markets to reach a return on capital employed commensurate with the target figures set by the Competition Commission as amended by subsequent economic circumstances (for example inflation and divided yield targets). The dividend target is based on the average yield of 3.23%[1].

In the tables which follow, we have given each line in each table a reference, and the source of each calculation is shown, hopefully assisting readers to understand the methodology more clearly and for non-accountants to understand how the various measures are calculated.

---

[1] *Dividend yield for FTSE250 companies, July 2024.*

2. The Balance Sheet

As a result, the balance sheet for the businesses at 31 March 2024 might be as shown in Table A below.

Ref	Item (£000)	Derivation Ref	Shire	PTE	London
			£000	£000	£000
A1	Fixed Assets		18,167	23,101	16,390
A2	Current Assets		4,202	4,864	7,338
A3	Total Assets	A1+A2	22,369	27,965	23,728
A4	Current Liabilities		4,491	5,133	8,063
A5	Net Current Assets	A2-A4	(289)	(269)	(725)
A6	Total assets less current liabilities	A3-A5	17,878	22,832	15,665
A7	Long term liabilities		9,594	11,340	3,175
A8	**Net Assets**	A3-A4-A7	**8,284**	**11,492**	**12,490**
A9	Shares		2,035	2,715	2,513
A10	Retained profits		3,419	1,496	3,826
A11	Reserves		2,830	7,281	6,152
A12	Shareholders' funds	(Sum A9:A11)	**8,284**	**11,492**	**12,490**

3. Target Returns

The target return will typically comprise the following elements:

- Traditional inflation-free rate of interest for risk-free loans
- Expected rate of inflation
- The risk of defaulting on a loan (which will typically be fixed in the range 0-5 per cent, depending on the risk assessment)
- The risk profile of a particular company, venture or project: this will be priced between 0% and 50% or, in some cases, even higher.

In regulated industries such as utilities, the permitted levels of return are the most difficult to determine, and the most hotly contested.

The key assumptions we have used in this modelling exercise are based on the Competition Commission's view of bus industry profit levels in the light of the operators' weighted average cost of capital (WACC), but using updated financial targets.

However, it must be emphasised that these assumptions on returns remain controversial, and are not necessarily accepted by the operators, especially in the light of the significant changes that have taken place in the bus market over the years since the Commission started its investigation in 2010. Apart from anything else, these changes – including the impact of Covid – are likely to mean that bus operations, particularly in a deregulated environment, may very well have a much higher perceived risk rating than the Commission allowed. Nevertheless, the Commission's view represents a useful starting point for this analysis.

Table B: Key Financial Assumptions

Ref	Item	Derivation Ref	Shire	PTE	London
B1	Inflation Assumption		2.40%	2.40%	2.40%
B2	Return on shareholders' funds (real)		7.00%	7.00%	7.00%
B3	Interest payable (on net debt) (real)		6.00%	6.00%	6.00%
B4	Corporation Tax Rate		25.00%	25.00%	25.00%
B5	Nominal return on capital	B1+B2	9.40%	9.40%	9.40%
B6	Nominal interest rate on net debt	B1+B3	8.40%	8.40%	8.40%

We can therefore estimate the level of net profit the company should be making (i.e., after tax) based on the target rates of return on assets, and the assumed levels of interest payments that will need to be met. It is also possible to model the level of Corporation Tax the business would be paying.

4. Balance Sheet Analysis and Target Net Profits

From this structure, it is possible to derive the key information about the companies' financial position shown in Table C below, and these then drive the target profit levels.

Table C: Notional Bus Companies' Balance Sheet Analysis

Ref	Item	Derivation Ref	Shire	PTE	London
			£000	£000	£000
C1	Net debt	A7 + A4 - A2	9,883	11,609	3,900
C2	Annual repayment	C1/5	1,977	2,322	780
C3	Interest costs	B6 * C1	830	975	328
C4	Target net profit	B5 * A12	779	1,080	1,174
C5	Target dividend	B7 * A12	268	371	403
C6	Capital Employed	A3 - A4	17,878	22,832	15,665

5. Operating Costs

Having calculated the amount of money the business needs to earn to meet its obligations and give its shareholders a fair return, we can then relate that to the costs of actually running the service.

The following figures are based on the actual operating ratios for different cost items derived from regular monitoring of industry costs and operating KPIs.

First, we look at the operating assumptions for our 200 vehicle companies in Table D. These will give us the operating statistics shown in Table E. Finally, we calculate that the cost of provision of bus services in accordance with these statistics, which would be as shown in Table F below.

Table D: Notional Bus Companies: Key Operating Assumptions

Ref	Item	Units	Shire	PTE	London
D1	Fleet	Vehicles	200.0	200.0	200.0
D2	Peak Requirement	Vehicles	175.0	175.0	175.0
D3	Average speed	Km/hour	19.7	18.0	12.2
D4	Average bus hours/day	Hours	11.5	12.2	15.6
D5	Full operating days/year	Days	363.0	363.0	363.0
D6	Fuel consumption	Km/litre	2.57	2.46	2.37
D7	Driver to bus hours ratio	:1	1.18	1.32	1.24
D8	Working week	Hours	39.7	40.0	44.4
D9	Other staff	Per Bus	0.6	0.6	0.6
D10	Unit Labour cost	£/year	39,080	38,500	56,000
D11	Unit fuel cost (gross)	£/litre	1.09	1.09	1.09
D12	Unit oil & tyres cost	£/km	0.024	0.024	0.024
D13	Engineering costs	£/Bus hour	2.20	2.15	2.39
D14	Overheads	£/PVR	36.00	35.00	25.25
D15	Claims & Insurance	£/PVR	6.50	5.20	8.20
D16	SV Costs	£/PVR	8.80	9.05	9.20

Table E: Resulting Operating Statistics

Ref	Item	Units	Derivation Ref	Shires	PTE	London
E1	Vehicle utilisation	Bus Hrs/year	D4 * D5	4,185	4,432	5,652
E2	Vehicle utilisation	Km/year	E1 * D3	82,410	79,647	68,897
E3	Annual utilisation	Bus hours	E1 * D2	732,443	775,640	989,084
E4	Payroll time	Man hours	E4 * D7	864,283	1,023,845	1,226,464
E5	Weekly time	Man hours	E4/52	16,621	19,689	23,586
E6	Staff needed	Drivers	E5 / D8	418	492	531
E7	Other workforce	People	D9 * D2	124	128	124
E8	KM Run	Million km	E2 * D2	14.4	13.9	12.1
E9	Total fuel used	Litres (m)	E8 / D6	5.6	5.7	5.1

Table F: Calculation of Operating Costs

Ref	Item	Derivation Ref	Shires	PTE	London
			£000	£000	£000
F1	Labour	(E6 + E7) * D10	21,191	23,879	36,692
F2	Fuel	E9 * D11	6,109	6,168	5,538
F3	Oil & Tyres	E8 * D12	346	335	289
F4	Maintenance	E3 * D13	1,610	1,668	2,368
F5	Overheads	D2 * D14	6,300	6,125	4,419
F6	Semi-Variable Costs	D2 * D16	1,540	1,584	1,610
F7	Claims	D2 * D15	1,138	910	1,435
F8	Leasing	Unit Cost	323	623	1,662
F9	**Total Operating Costs**		38,233	40,669	54,014
F10	Depreciation	% of assets	2,613	2,634	1,843
F11	**TOTAL COSTS**		40,846	43,303	55,857

6. The Target Revenue

Having determined the costs of operation, it is therefore possible to calculate the level of revenue which the company would need to earn to deliver the financial targets we have set.

This will include the need to undertake capital investment during the year to replace life-expired assets and to enable the company to continue in business (which we call "replacement investment"). The company will have to find the cash required and will need to generate the money from its earnings. We have assessed the need for such expenditure based on the expected lives of the vehicles operated and other investment required in buildings, fixtures and equipment. The calculations are shown in Table G below.

Table G: Calculation of Revenue Targets

Ref	Item	Derivation Ref	Shires	PTE	London
			£000	£000	£000
G1	Target net profit	C4	779	1,080	1,174
G2	Tax	@ 25%	260	360	391
G3	Pre-Tax Profit Target	G1 + G2	1,038	1,440	1,565
G4	Interest costs	C3	830	975	328
G5	Target Operating Surplus	G3 + G4	1,868	2,416	1,893
G6	Operating costs	F9	38,233	40,669	54,014
G7	Capex requirement	Asset Cost	5,796	7,849	1,631
G8	**Target Revenue**	G5 + G6 + G7	**45,898**	**50,933**	**57,538**

We have taken the starting point to be the company's need to make replacement investments rather than the more conventional provision for depreciation. Depreciation in the accounts is designed to make provision for future replacement of assets: in practice, however, this is based on the historic value of the original asset and not the expenditure required to replace it. This is a particular issue at present with the need to replace life-expired diesel buses with much more expensive battery electric or fuel-cell vehicles. Whilst additional finance can be obtained, any business must maintain the availability of credit by always meeting its obligations and fulfilling credit providers' financial criteria.

7. The Profit and Loss Account

If these targets were to be achieved, the companies would have profit and loss accounts similar to those shown in Table H below, whilst the performance measures which the companies would thereby deliver are shown in Table I.

Note that in the P&L in Table H we revert to the standard depreciation figure, which increases both the pre-tax profit and the tax liability when compared with the target figures in Table G.

Table H: Notional Bus Companies' Target P&L Accounts

Ref	Item	Derivation Ref	Shires	PTE	London
			£000	£000	£000
H1	Revenue	G8	45,898	50,933	57,538
H2	Operating Costs	F9	38,233	40,669	54,014
H3	**EBITDA**	H1-H2	7,665	10,264	3,524
H4	Depreciation/Amortisation	F10	2,613	2,634	1,843
H5	**EBIT (Operating Profit)**	H3-H4	5,052	7,630	1,682
H6	Interest	C3	830	975	328
H7	**Pre-Tax Profit**	H5-H6	4,222	6,655	1,354
H8	Tax	H7 * 25%	1,055	1,664	338
H9	**Net profit for year**	H7-H8	3,166	4,991	1,015
H10	Dividend	C5	268	371	403
H11	**Retained profit**	H9-H10	2,899	4,620	612

Table I: Notional Bus Companies' Performance Indicators

Ref	Item	Derivation Ref	Shires	Mets	London
I1	EBITDA margin	H3 / H1	16.7%	20.2%	6.1%
I2	Operating Profit margin (EBIT)	H5 / H1	11.0%	15.0%	2.9%
I3	Return on Capital Employed	H5 / C6	28.3%	33.4%	10.7%
I4	Pre-Tax Profit Margin	H7 / H1	9.2%	13.1%	2.4%
I5	Return on Shareholders' funds	H9 / A12	38.2%	43.4%	8.1%
I6	Return on Fixed Assets	H9 / A1	17.4%	21.6%	6.2%
I7	Total Assets	A3	22,369	27,965	23,728
I8	Return on Total Assets	H9 / I8	14.2%	17.8%	4.3%
I9	Revenue per bus (£000)	H1 / D2	262	291	329
I10	Revenue per bus hour (£)	H1 / E3	63	66	58

8. Cashflow Movements and Net Debt Analysis

Having achieved these results, it is then possible to analyse the resulting cashflow, in the "source and application of funds" analysis and the movement in the companies' net debt position. This is done in Table J.

It will be seen that all three companies would have earned enough monies to allow them to reduce their net debt – which would be the prudent thing to do in the current economic climate and in an "on target" year. This gives the company the headroom and financial strength to borrow more when it needs to in order to expand or withstand difficult times when profits fall below target levels.

Table J: Cashflow & Net Debt Analysis

Ref	Item	Derivation Ref	Shires	PTE	London
			£000	£000	£000
J1	Income from operations	H1	45,898	50,933	57,538
J2	less operating costs	H2	40,846	43,303	55,857
J3	Net revenue from operations (EBIT)	H5	5,052	7,630	1,682
J4	Tax on EBIT	H8	(1,055)	(1,664)	(338)
J5	Depreciation provision	H4	2,613	2,634	1,843
J6	Capital Expenditure	G7	(5,796)	(7,849)	(1,631)
J7	Cash return on capital employed	Sum (J3:J6)	813	752	1,555
J8	Capital employed	C6	17,878	22,832	15,665
J9	% cash return on capital employed	J7/J8	4.5%	3.3%	9.9%
Distribution of free cashflow					
J10	Dividend	C5	268	371	403
J11	Interest costs	H6	830	975	328
J12	Debt repayment	C2	1,977	2,322	780
J13	Total cash outflow	Sum (J10:J12)	3,074	3,668	1,511
J14	Net cash position	J7 - J13	(2,261)	(2,916)	43
Analysis of Net Debt					
J15	Opening net debt	C1	9,883	11,609	3,900
J16	Additional borrowing required	J13	2,261	2,916	(43)
J17	Debt repaid	J12	1,977	2,322	780
J18	Closing net debt	Sum (J15:J17)	10,167	12,203	3,077

9. Drivers of Profit Levels

Returns will vary between operators and between different parts of the country for all sorts of reasons, including:

- The value of the assets on the balance sheet: the higher the value, the higher the cash profit needed to meet the target return. This will be affected by whether assets are owned or leased, and whether they are held on the balance sheets of subsidiaries or holding companies.

- Investment levels and aspirations: the mixture between equity funding (from shareholders) and debt (provided by lenders such as bond holders or banks), which will also affect the levels of return required (the "Weighted Average Cost of Capital", or WACC).

- The perceived risk profile of the business: the higher the perceived risks (from competition, for example, or length of contract in the case of tendered services), the higher the interest rate that will have to be paid to lenders or bond holders.

- The level of operating costs: because the target profit levels are based on returns on asset value and not margins, they will be a fixed cash item – so that where costs vary (as for example between London and the rest of the country), profit margins will be different.

- Other financial obligations that a company would need to meet from the excess of income over expenditure. Typically, at present, this would include extra contributions to pension schemes and any unfunded pension obligations. Where extra pension payments are necessary, the sum required needs to be added to the revenue target and would therefore boost the apparent operating profit margin.

Using the modelling in the worked example, scenario testing suggests that each 1.0% added to target returns and interest rates paid increases the required operating margin by approximately 0.7%.

It will be seen that, based on the calculations and assumptions we have made, the current profit margins of bus companies are below the levels that we would expect a regulator to allow on the basis of the asset base and fair returns needed to run a successful bus company.

As we pointed out in section 2 above, companies' balance sheets currently vary widely. Despite this, the conclusion must be that current profit levels appear to be too low.

10. Profit Distribution

It is also important to appreciate that the fact a company makes "an operating profit" does **not** mean that the money made is automatically available for the shareholders. This money must be used to:

- pay its Corporation Tax bill
- pay interest on its borrowings
- repay the loans it has taken out
- to provide for reserves to enable the company to survive in the bad times

Only after that can it pay dividends to reward shareholders for their ownership and risk.

Given that our three example businesses achieve their targets, we can show what would happen to that money, and this is illustrated in Table K together with Figure 1.

It will be seen that, in the English Shires, only 5.3% of the amount is actually paid to shareholders, with around 21% going in tax, 16% in interest payments and 39% in repayment of debt, leaving a balance of 18% for transfer to the reserves.

In London, the differences in the business model are seen in the different distribution of the much lower available profits – with similar dividend payments in cash terms representing a higher proportion (around 24%) of the cash profits made.

Table K: Analysis of What Happens to Profits

Ref	Item	Derivation Ref	Shires	PTE	London
Cash Breakdown			£000	£000	£000
K1	Interest	J11	830	975	328
K2	Tax	J4	1,055	1,664	338
K3	Debt repaid	J12	1,977	2,322	780
K4	Dividends	J10	268	371	403
K5	Transfer to/(from) reserves	H3 – Sum (K1:K4)	922	2,298	(168)
K6	**Total**	Sum (K1:K6)	**5,052**	**7,630**	**1,682**
Percentage Breakdown					
K7	Interest		16.4%	12.8%	19.5%
K8	Tax		20.9%	21.8%	20.1%
K9	Debt repaid		39.1%	30.4%	46.4%
K10	Dividends		5.3%	4.9%	24.0%
K11	Reinvestment		18.3%	30.1%	(10.0%)
K12	Total		16.4%	12.8%	19.5%

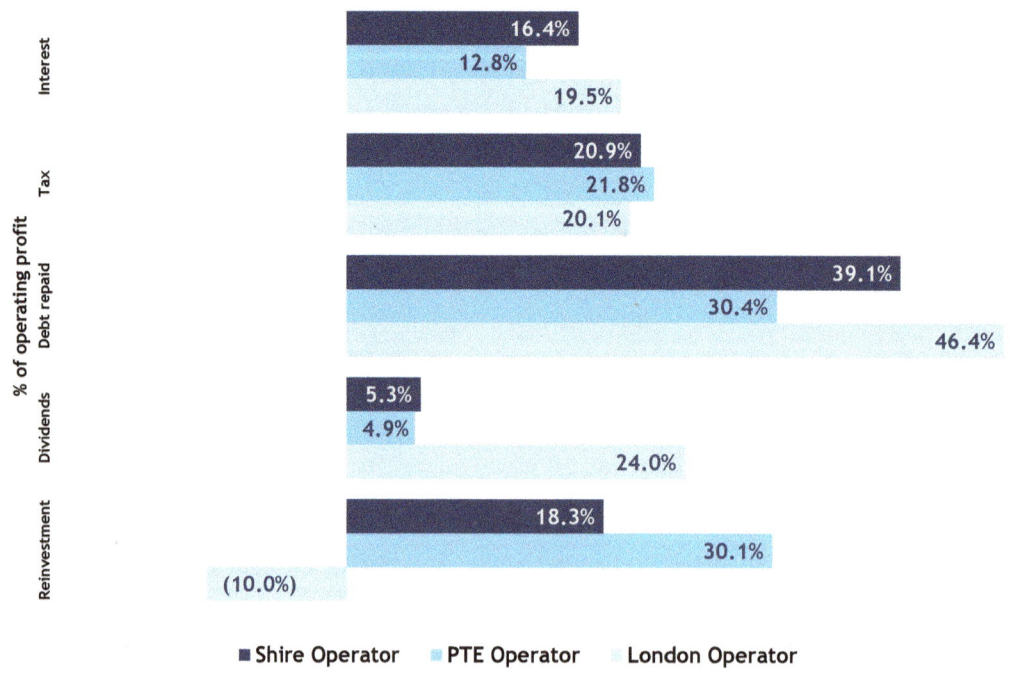

Figure 1: Percentage Breakdown of Operating Profit Distribution

11. The Effect of Operating Leases

The biggest change in financial structure as a result of London-style tendering might well be the move to operating leases for vehicles – as has indeed happened in the TfL regime.

The system of operating leases means that the ownership of the vehicle remains with the leasing company (lessor) – so it does not appear on the company's books, and therefore neither does any loan which might be required to fund the purchase.

Instead, a periodic (monthly or quarterly) lease payment is made to the lessor which covers three elements of the costs – initial capital cost, interest costs and the depreciation of the asset. The accounting consequences are summarised in Table 12 below.

The effect of using vehicles on operating lease is to:

- Reduce the capital employed and therefore the target profit
- Reduce the company's financing costs
- Increase the operating costs by the amount of the lease payment.

In comparing the two approaches, it is likely that the cost of (c) will be equivalent to or even slightly greater than the savings made from (a) and (b). Thus, the revenue which must be raised from fares or a tendering authority will be the same, but the operating profit – and therefore the margin – will appear to be lower.

On expiry of the operating lease, the vehicle will be returned to lessor, who can then either lease it to somebody else, or sell it on, recording a profit or loss on sale of asset on disposal in the leasing company's P&L.

Table 12: Accounting Effects of Owned and Leased Model for Buses

Item	Owned Model	Leased Model
Fixed Asset Value	On Operator Balance Sheet	On Lessor Balance Sheet
Borrowing to fund purchase	Shown as liability on operator balance sheet	Shown as liability on lessor balance sheet
Depreciation	Charged to Operator P&L	Asset depreciated by lessor, charged to lessee as part of overall leasing payment, charged to operating costs.
Borrowing costs	Charged to P&L as part of overall financing costs. This is not charged to operating profit, but to pre-tax profit.	Rolled into overall leasing payment, charged to operating costs
Residual Value	On disposal of the asset, the proceeds of sale are compared with the book value, with any difference charged/credited to the P&L as profit/loss on sale of assets.	The lessor will dispose of the asset on expiry and accept either the profit (or the loss) into its own P&L account. The likely residual value will be factored into the overall leasing cost during the life of the asset.

A Worked Example

Using the worked example of a bus company operating in a PTE area discussed above, we can illustrate the effects of the switch. In a 200-vehicle company with an average fleet age of 7.6 years, the target revenue required in order to achieve the appropriate return on capital employed is £50.9m. The chart at Figure 2 below shows the effect of running the company with leased or owned vehicles.

In the leased option:

- the operating costs are £3.7m higher to meet the leasing costs
- the depreciation charges are much lower
- the level of operating profit *seems* to be lower, at £6.1m
- the operating margin is 12.1%
- the capital employed by the company is £3.4m giving a minimum target net profit of £0.44m to meet obligations to lenders and shareholders.

Under the owned model:

- operating costs are £3.7m a year lower
- depreciation charges are £2.3m higher
- because operating profit is calculated before interest costs, it appears to be higher, too, at £7.6m
- the operating margin is much higher at 15.0%
- the capital employed by the company is almost six times higher at £22.8m, giving a minimum net profit target of £1.1m to meet its obligations.

This example illustrates the danger of designing a model based on purely on assumed operating profit margins. The determining factor is not the margin, but the capital employed by the operating company and the achievement of a target return on that capital. In this example, the leased model shows an operating margin of 12.2%, whilst the owned model shows one of 15.1% - but the cost to the passengers or the tendering authority would remain unchanged at £50.6m. Note that the figures in the panel and on the diagram are rounded.

Figure 2: Costs and Profit Breakdown with Leased or Owned Vehicles

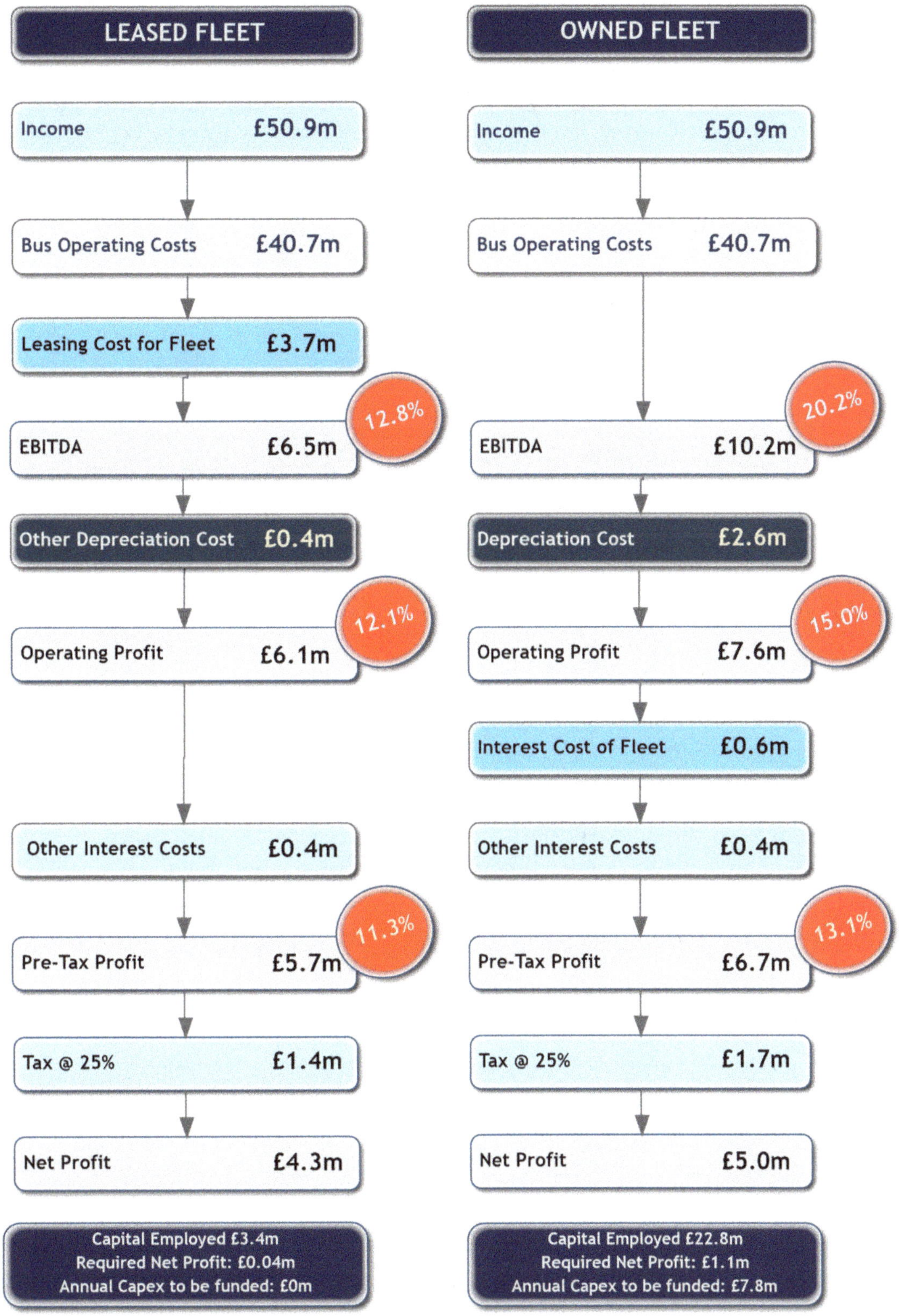

LEASED FLEET

- Income: £50.9m
- Bus Operating Costs: £40.7m
- Leasing Cost for Fleet: £3.7m
- EBITDA: £6.5m (12.8%)
- Other Depreciation Cost: £0.4m
- Operating Profit: £6.1m (12.1%)
- Other Interest Costs: £0.4m
- Pre-Tax Profit: £5.7m (11.3%)
- Tax @ 25%: £1.4m
- Net Profit: £4.3m

Capital Employed £3.4m
Required Net Profit: £0.04m
Annual Capex to be funded: £0m

OWNED FLEET

- Income: £50.9m
- Bus Operating Costs: £40.7m
- EBITDA: £10.2m (20.2%)
- Depreciation Cost: £2.6m
- Operating Profit: £7.6m (15.0%)
- Interest Cost of Fleet: £0.6m
- Other Interest Costs: £0.4m
- Pre-Tax Profit: £6.7m (13.1%)
- Tax @ 25%: £1.7m
- Net Profit: £5.0m

Capital Employed £22.8m
Required Net Profit: £1.1m
Annual Capex to be funded: £7.8m

EBITDA stands for "Earnings before Depreciation, Amortisation, Interest and Taxation"

Appendix B: Bus Speeds – A Worked Example

1. Introduction

The key variables in driving the cost of our bus routes are therefore **time** and **speed**. Some costs, particularly fuel, oil and tyres, will also depend on **distance** – though of course fuel consumption is also influenced to a measurable extent by speed.

> **Speed Assumptions**
>
> An urban bus route runs for around 3½ miles (6 km) between the town centre and a local suburb - a round trip of 12 km. The service runs every ten minutes (six departures per hour) between 0600 and 1900 and every 20 minutes from 1900 to midnight.
>
> Recent research suggests that a well-performing network in relatively uncongested traffic can achieve an average speed of 12.0 mph (19.3 kph). Narrow roads and frequent stops might mean a fall to 10.3mph (16.5 kph). More serious congestion could drive it down to 9.5 mph (15.2 kph), or even lower (bus speeds in London average below 8 mph).

> **The Difference that Speed Makes**
>
> - At 12 mph, our 12 km route will take 37 minutes to run a trip from the town centre to the outer terminus and back again. This means that would require 4 buses during the day.
>
> - At 10.3 mph, the time will rise to 44 minutes. The route will now need 5 buses, with one extra needed to cover the extra time and maintain the frequency.
>
> - At 9.5 mph. the time rises to 47 minutes, and the uncertainties of traffic congestion lead the operator to increase recovery time to 4 minutes per trip. This means that 6 buses will now be required to run the 10-minute frequency.
>
> Clearly, the slowest journey needs significantly more resources to deliver the same frequency and will therefore be much more expensive to operate. We will discuss these costs and how they work later in the chapter.

2. Calculating the Resources Needed

Having established what governs the resources needed to run a bus service (time, speed and distance), it is possible to calculate the level of resources, or inputs, that will be required to operate a given route. From there, we can calculate the cost of providing the service.

The figures we need to know are:

- The time taken from one end of the route to the other and back again.
- The hours of operation

- The frequency of operation
- The distance travelled.

From this information, we can calculate:

- the number of vehicles we need
- the number of drivers we will need to employ (allowing of course for sickness and holidays).
- the distance each bus will cover and therefore how much fuel and oil will be needed, and the number of tyres used.

> ### Calculating the Resources Needed
>
> Looking at the town service we discussed earlier in the chapter, we have established that the route runs every ten minutes from 0600 in the morning until 1900, and then every 20 minutes from 1900 until 2400, seven days a week.
>
> At 12 mph:
>
> - Two buses will work for 18 hours day and two will work for 13 hours a day, a total of 62 bus hours a day. If the service runs for 363 days a year, the annual total will be 22,506.
> - Paid staff hours, allowing for sickness, holidays, and unexpected absence, would total 29,258.
> - Between them, the buses will cover 1,116 km per day. The annual figure would be 405,000.
>
> At 10.3 mph:
>
> - Two buses will work for 18 hours a day and three for 13. A total of 80 bus hours, amounting to 29,040 per annum (29% more).
> - Paid hours would be 37,752 (also up 29%).
> - The distance run would remain the same.
>
> At 9.5 mph:
>
> - three buses will work for 18 hours a day and three for 13. Bus hours rise to 93 per day, 33,759 per annum (up 50% from base case).
> - Paid hours would be 50,639 (also up 50%).
> - Again, the distance run would be the same.
>
> These are the key inputs that will enable us to calculate the costs of operation of our route.

3. The Impact on Costs

The annual cost of operating our sample service can be calculated using the data we now have about the resources required alongside available unit cost information taken from the CPT Cost Monitor.

Our model then calculates the expected cost of operating our route at the three different speeds. Our current estimate that the operator needs to make an operating profit of 7.5% to meet their financial obligations. This figure enables us to estimate what the annual cash profit needs to be and see how it changes with the speed of the service. The increase in profit is needed to fund the extra equipment required to run the service at the slower speeds.

Once we have a target revenue figure, we can also estimate the number of passengers we will need to carry to achieve that target.

If we add the profit needed to the costs of operation, we know how much revenue we need to earn from passengers. If we know the typical average fare per passenger, we can also calculate how many passengers we need to carry each year to achieve our targets. Nationally, the average revenue per passenger in 2022/23 was £1.61. Let us assume that our service earns a similar figure.

The results of these calculations are shown in Table A below.

Table A: Cost and Revenue Estimates at Different Bus Speeds

Speed (mph)	12.0	10.3	9.5
	£000	£000	£000
Labour	844	1,047	1,250
Depreciation	91	113	135
Leasing	42	52	62
Overheads	113	141	168
Fuel	172	172	172
Parts	60	75	89
Claims	36	45	54
	1,358	1,644	1,929
Target Operating Profit	143	173	203
Target Revenue	1,501	1,816	2,132
Annual Patronage Required at constant average fare (000s)	933	1,130	1,326

Appendix C: BSIP Funding Allocations (England)

1. Introduction

As noted in the main text (Chapter 4), the initial allocation of BSIP funding was made in April 2022, when a total of £1 billion was awarded to 31 LTAs around the country. The awards covered the three financial years 2022/23, 2023/24 and 2024/25. Subsequently, a further announcement was made the DfT made available a funding package designed to last from July 2023 until March 2025, at a total cost of £300m, including a £160m allocation to all LTAs to assist with the implementation of their improvement plans. This was initially known as BSIP+, then renamed BSIP Phase 2). A further £700m in BSIP funding was promised for local authorities in the North as part of the Network North announcement made following the decision to abandon Phase 2 of the HS2 project north of Birmingham.

2. Funding Allocations to 2025

The full listing of LTAs and the amounts they have been allocated by DfT can be seen in Table A below.

The initial tranche saw £534m (49.3%) allocated to the Combined Authorities, with £296m (27.3%) to the remaining County Councils and £254m (23.4%) to the unitary authorities.

In the BSIP+ allocations across the two years, £28m went to the Combined Authorities (17.8%), £69m (44.3%) to the counties and £60m (37.9%) to the unitary councils.

In the third round, allocated from the Network North funds made available after the cancellation of the HS2 leg to Manchester, £150m was split between authorities in the Midlands and the North. Once again, the lion's share went to the Combined Authorities, who received £78.0m (52%), with the counties receiving £36.6m (24.3%) and the unitary authorities £35.6m (23.7%).

Overall, spending allocations per capita averaged £39.80 across all LTAs, but there was wide variation between authority types here too, between £43.16 in the Combined Authority areas, £21.75 in the counties and £26.16 in the unitary authority areas. The highest per capita allocation went to Portsmouth City (£233.74), followed by the North East Combined Authority (£155.21) and Reading (£151.66).

In the original three-year settlement, the average allocation per head in the 32 authorities was £23.17, with the same wide variation between authority types. The figures were £36.02 in the Combined Authority areas, £15.90 in the counties and £19.03 in the unitary authority areas.

Table A: BSIP Funding Allocations (£000)
Local Transport Authorities in England

Authority	Original BSIP 2022-2025	BSIP+ 2024-25	BSIP+ 2023-24	BSIP 3 2024-25	Total Allocation	Total Allocation Per Capita	Round 1 Allocation per Capita
Bedford Borough Council	0.00	546.76	546.76	0.00	1,093.51	5.89	0.00
Blackburn with Darwen Borough Council	3,722.32	470.17	470.17	880.00	5,542.66	35.78	24.03
Blackpool Council	0.00	506.49	506.49	802.00	1,814.98	12.88	0.00
Bournemouth, Christchurch and Poole Council	8,858.43	617.51	617.51	0.00	10,093.45	25.23	22.14
Bracknell Forest Council	0.00	325.72	325.72	0.00	651.43	5.20	0.00
Brighton and Hove City Council	27,854.33	0.00	0.00	0.00	27,854.33	100.80	100.80
Buckinghamshire Council	0.00	1,310.33	1,310.33	0.00	2,620.67	4.72	0.00
Cambridgeshire and Peterborough CA	0.00	2,314.17	2,314.17	0.00	4,628.34	5.16	0.00
Central Bedfordshire Council	3,724.72	350.46	350.46	0.00	4,425.63	14.97	12.60
Cheshire East Council	0.00	1,187.60	1,187.60	2,268.00	4,643.19	11.59	0.00
Cheshire West and Chester Council	0.00	1,291.07	1,291.07	2,031.00	4,613.14	12.90	0.00
City of York Council	17,360.00	0.00	0.00	1,153.00	18,513.00	91.80	86.08
Cornwall Council (including Isles of Scilly)	13,307.92	1,969.16	1,969.16	0.00	17,246.25	30.15	23.27
Cumberland Council	0.00	464.74	464.74	1,554.00	2,483.49	9.07	0.00
Derby City Council	7,024.65	323.61	323.61	1,486.00	9,157.86	35.07	26.90

Authority	Original BSIP 2022-2025	BSIP+ 2024-25	BSIP+ 2023-24	BSIP 3 2024-25	Total Allocation	Total Allocation Per Capita	Round 1 Allocation per Capita
Derbyshire County Council	47,003.44	0.00	0.00	4,519.00	51,522.44	64.66	58.99
Devon County Council	14,057.27	1,677.39	1,677.39	0.00	17,412.06	21.38	17.26
Dorset Council	0.00	884.22	884.22	0.00	1,768.44	4.64	0.00
East Riding of Yorkshire Council	0.00	1,141.58	1,141.58	1,946.00	4,229.15	12.32	0.00
East Sussex County Council	41,415.03	0.00	0.00	0.00	41,415.03	75.72	75.72
Essex County Council	0.00	4,890.98	4,890.98	0.00	9,781.95	6.49	0.00
Gloucestershire County Council	0.00	2,209.62	2,209.62	0.00	4,419.25	6.83	0.00
Greater Manchester Combined Authority	94,800.00	0.00	0.00	16,309.00	111,109.00	38.74	33.05
Hampshire County Council	0.00	3,579.46	3,579.46	0.00	7,158.92	5.09	0.00
Herefordshire Council	0.00	952.04	952.04	1,064.00	2,968.07	15.82	0.00
Hertfordshire County Council	29,732.10	1,488.38	1,488.38	0.00	32,708.86	27.24	24.76
Hull City Council	0.00	756.53	756.53	1,519.00	3,032.06	11.38	0.00
Isle of Wight Council	0.00	290.03	290.03	0.00	580.05	4.12	0.00
Kent County Council	35,070.14	2,301.40	2,301.40	0.00	39,672.93	25.13	22.22
Lancashire County Council	30,444.38	2,247.18	2,247.18	0.00	34,938.74	28.27	24.63
Leicester City Council	0.00	727.29	727.29	2,096.00	3,550.58	9.70	0.00
Leicestershire County Council	0.00	1,788.51	1,788.51	4,051.00	7,628.03	10.70	0.00
Lincolnshire County Council	0.00	2,120.28	2,120.28	4,370.00	8,610.56	11.19	0.00
Liverpool City Region Combined Authority	12,294.40	3,119.12	3,119.12	8,825.00	27,357.63	17.63	7.92

Authority	Original BSIP 2022-2025	BSIP+ 2024-25	BSIP+ 2023-24	BSIP 3 2024-25	Total Allocation	Total Allocation Per Capita	Round 1 Allocation per Capita
Luton Borough Council	19,145.10	0.00	0.00	0.00	19,145.10	85.16	85.16
Medway Council	0.00	768.78	768.78	0.00	1,537.56	5.49	0.00
Milton Keynes Council	0.00	654.19	654.19	0.00	1,308.39	4.54	0.00
Norfolk County Council	49,552.02	0.00	0.00	0.00	49,552.02	53.96	53.96
North East Combined Authority	163,521.17	0.00	0.00	11,202.00	174,723.17	155.21	145.26
North East Lincolnshire Council	4,684.75	280.13	280.13	893.00	6,138.01	39.05	29.80
North Lincolnshire Council	0.00	547.38	547.38	965.00	2,059.76	12.12	0.00
North Northamptonshire Council	0.00	569.41	569.41	2,045.00	3,183.82	8.76	0.00
North Yorkshire Council	0.00	1,463.69	1,463.69	3,500.00	6,427.38	10.39	0.00
Nottingham City Council	11,367.41	445.02	445.02	1,840.00	14,097.46	44.11	35.57
Nottinghamshire County Council	18,713.80	1,210.43	1,210.43	4,691.00	25,825.66	31.26	22.65
Oxfordshire County Council	12,704.92	963.74	963.74	0.00	14,632.40	20.14	17.49
Plymouth City Council	0.00	816.56	816.56	0.00	1,633.13	6.17	0.00
Portsmouth City Council	48,344.70	0.00	0.00	0.00	48,344.70	233.74	233.74
Reading Borough Council	26,263.60	0.00	0.00	0.00	26,263.60	151.66	151.66
Royal Borough of Windsor and Maidenhead	0.00	437.12	437.12	0.00	874.23	5.68	0.00
Rutland County Council	0.00	253.28	253.28	233.00	739.56	17.87	0.00
Shropshire Council	0.00	1,490.49	1,490.49	1,840.00	4,820.98	14.85	0.00
Slough Borough Council	0.00	343.27	343.27	0.00	686.53	4.34	0.00

Authority	Original BSIP 2022-2025	BSIP+ 2024-25	BSIP+ 2023-24	BSIP 3 2024-25	Total Allocation	Total Allocation Per Capita	Round 1 Allocation per Capita
Somerset Council	11,855.86	737.08	737.08	0.00	13,330.02	23.26	20.69
South Yorkshire Mayoral Combined Authority	0.00	3,151.35	3,151.35	7,820.00	14,122.71	10.28	0.00
Southampton City Council	0.00	639.58	639.58	0.00	1,279.15	5.17	0.00
Southend-on-Sea City Council	0.00	479.25	479.25	0.00	958.50	5.31	0.00
Staffordshire County Council	0.00	1,327.67	1,327.67	4,982.00	7,637.35	8.70	0.00
Stoke-on-Trent City Council	31,663.50	0.00	0.00	1,469.00	33,132.50	128.40	122.71
Suffolk County Council	0.00	1,878.43	1,878.43	0.00	3,756.85	4.92	0.00
Surrey County Council	0.00	3,923.92	3,923.92	0.00	7,847.84	6.51	0.00
Swindon Borough Council	0.00	415.83	415.83	0.00	831.66	3.56	0.00
Tees Valley Combined Authority	0.00	1,529.48	1,529.48	3,851.00	6,909.95	12.12	0.00
Telford and Wrekin Council	0.00	650.94	650.94	1,055.00	2,356.88	12.68	0.00
Thurrock Council	0.00	432.86	432.86	0.00	865.71	4.92	0.00
Torbay Council	0.00	403.92	403.92	0.00	807.85	5.79	0.00
Warrington Borough Council	16,198.42	0.00	0.00	1,200.00	17,398.42	82.37	76.69
Warwickshire County Council	0.00	2,072.25	2,072.25	3,394.00	7,538.50	12.58	0.00
West Berkshire Council	2,596.73	239.04	239.04	0.00	3,074.81	19.00	16.04
West Midlands Combined Authority	87,857.76	0.00	0.00	16,604.00	104,461.76	35.82	30.13
West Northamptonshire Council	0.00	687.11	687.11	2,421.00	3,795.22	8.85	0.00
West of England Combined Authority	105,488.50	0.00	0.00	0.00	105,488.50	90.03	90.03

Authority	Original BSIP 2022-2025	BSIP+ 2024-25	BSIP+ 2023-24	BSIP 3 2024-25	Total Allocation	Total Allocation Per Capita	Round 1 Allocation per Capita
West Sussex County Council	17,401.60	1,102.40	1,102.40	0.00	19,606.40	22.15	19.66
West Yorkshire Combined Authority	69,974.07	3,875.22	3,875.22	13,373.00	91,097.51	38.77	29.78
Westmorland and Furness Council	0.00	412.13	412.13	1,289.00	2,113.26	9.31	0.00
Wiltshire Council	0.00	2,115.27	2,115.27	0.00	4,230.54	8.24	0.00
Wokingham Borough Council	0.00	401.32	401.32	0.00	802.64	4.50	0.00
Worcestershire County Council	0.00	1,429.69	1,429.69	3,433.00	6,292.37	10.40	0.00

Appendix D: Rural-Urban Classifications

1. The Origins

The rural urban classification system was developed by the Office for National Statistics and the Department of Food, Agriculture and Rural Affairs with assistance from Nottingham and Sheffield Universities.

2. Classifications

It is based on population densities and categorises census output areas (OAs), with six classifications, which are then built up into the local authority boundaries and other higher level classifications such as parliamentary constituencies or health districts. The classifications are:

a) Mainly Rural (rural including hub towns >=80%)

b) Largely Rural (rural including hub towns 50-79%)

c) Urban with Significant Rural (rural including hub towns 26-49%)

d) Urban with City and Town

e) Urban with Minor Conurbation

f) Urban with Major Conurbation

Hub towns mentioned in classifications (a), (b) and (c) are defined as small hub towns (population 10,000 to 30,000 people), which are treated as rural as they are an integral part of the wider rural area and provide a hub for services. The breakdown of the different classifications is shown in Table A below, whilst a map designed by the ONS can be found at Figure A below.

Table A: Rural-Urban Classification for Local Authority Districts
England, based on 2011 Census

Rural-urban category	Resident population	Percentage of Total
Predominantly rural	11,058,000	20.9
Mainly rural	4,723,000	8.9
Largely rural	6,335,000	11.9
Urban with significant rural	6,898,000	13.0
Predominantly urban	35,057,000	66.1
Urban with city and town	14,078,000	26.6
Urban with minor conurbation	2,107,000	4.0
Urban with major conurbation	18,872,000	35.6
Total England	53,013,000	100.0

Figure A: Map of Rural-Urban Classification for Local Authority Districts
ONS, England, based on 2011 Census

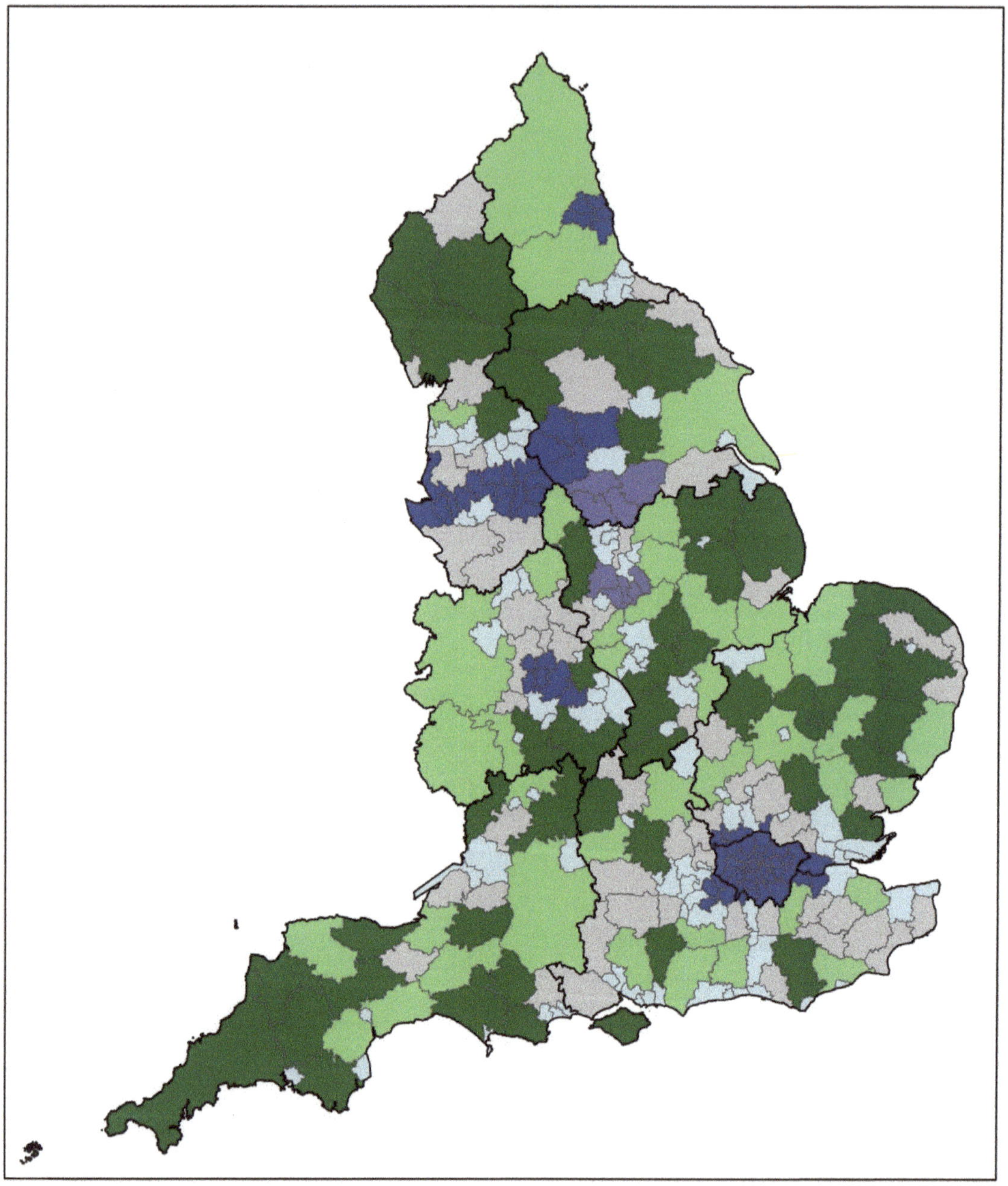

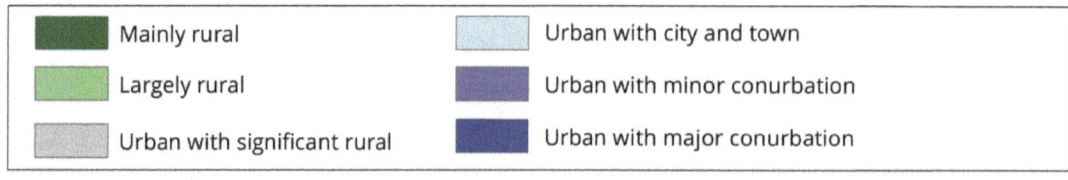

Rural-Urban Classification

- Mainly rural
- Largely rural
- Urban with significant rural
- Urban with city and town
- Urban with minor conurbation
- Urban with major conurbation

The Rural-Urban Classification for Local Authority Districts is a Government Statistical Service product developed by the Office for National Statistics and the Department for Environment, Food and Rural Affairs in collaboration with Sheffield and Nottingham Universities.

Source: Office for National Statistics licensed under the Open Government Licence v.3.0.   Contains OS data © Crown copyright 2017

Appendix E: Sector Financial Performance

1. Overview

This Appendix sets out the results of our analysis of sector financial performance between 2009/10 and 2022/23. Any differences of approach or assumptions made are included in the introduction to each sector.

2. London

The DfT does not publish statistics on operating costs in London. However, figures are available in the annual accounts of London Bus Services Ltd, the TfL subsidiary responsible for running the bus network. The figures include payments to operators, and LBSL's own expenses in planning and managing contracts. Figures on revenue are taken from the DfT's figures in sheet BUS05 but give a slightly lower revenue figure that reported in the LBSL accounts.

It will be seen that the figures show that the London network has run at an annual deficit since 2013/14, despite receipt of significant revenue support.

Table A: Local Bus Service Earnings, 2010-2023, London
£m, Constant (June 2023) Prices

Year to 31 March	Total Income	Operating Costs	Surplus/ (Deficit)	Margin (%)
2010	2,572.1	2,495.9	76.2	3.0%
2011	2,523.4	2,472.8	50.7	2.0%
2012	2,521.8	2,445.9	75.9	3.0%
2013	2,526.8	2,487.4	39.4	1.6%
2014	2,596.1	2,605.6	(9.5)	(0.4%)
2015	2,594.2	2,657.3	(63.1)	(2.4%)
2016	2,602.7	2,665.4	(62.8)	(2.4%)
2017	2,531.1	2,598.8	(67.7)	(2.7%)
2018	2,490.2	2,569.0	(78.8)	(3.2%)
2019	2,334.7	2,520.8	(186.1)	(8.0%)
2020	2,089.7	2,180.5	(90.8)	(4.3%)
2021	2,339.5	2,368.8	(29.3)	(1.3%)
2022	2,281.6	2,334.9	(53.4)	(2.3%)
2023	2,150.0	2,208.3	(58.3)	(2.7%)

3. English Metropolitan Areas

These figures cover bus operations within the Metropolitan Boroughs of England, where the former Passenger Transport Executives operated (which now form part of the Mayoral Combined Authorities, several of which now have extended boundaries. The operations cover the busiest conurbations outside London, including Greater Manchester, Merseyside, South Yorkshire, Tyne & Wear, West Midlands and West Yorkshire. The figures are taken directly from DfT statistics provided in Sheets BUS04 and BUS05.

It will be seen that the results in these areas have been hit particularly hard by Covid, with losses recorded since 2019/20 aside from the lockdown year when operating costs were much lower. Thanks to reductions in patronage and support spending, it will be seen that annual revenue fell by £482 million in real terms over the period (28%), whilst operating costs were reduced by £326m (21%) thanks largely to cuts in service levels.

Table B: Local Bus Service Earnings, 2010-2023, English Mets
£m, Constant (June 2023) Prices

Year to 31 March	Total Income	Operating Costs	Surplus/ (Deficit)	Margin (%)
2010	1,707.9	1,556.4	151.5	8.9%
2011	1,681.8	1,555.8	125.9	7.5%
2012	1,693.1	1,515.2	177.9	10.5%
2013	1,642.0	1,510.3	131.7	8.0%
2014	1,619.1	1,487.0	132.1	8.2%
2015	1,543.8	1,492.2	51.6	3.3%
2016	1,578.6	1,437.4	141.2	8.9%
2017	1,491.0	1,399.5	91.5	6.1%
2018	1,509.3	1,383.4	125.9	8.3%
2019	1,510.2	1,400.2	110.0	7.3%
2020	1,364.8	1,425.8	(60.9)	(4.5%)
2021	1,321.1	1,245.6	75.5	5.7%
2022	1,278.6	1,333.9	(55.3)	(4.3%)
2023	1,225.3	1,230.5	(5.2)	(0.4%)

4. English Shire Areas

More formally known as the "Non Metropolitan Areas", the Shires cover the rest of England outside London, and incorporate busy urban areas such as Bristol, Nottingham and Leicester as well as market towns and rural areas. Though some sub-division of service levels and patronage has been provided by DfT on service levels and patronage, these figures are not available for revenue or costs. The figures are taken directly from DfT statistics provided in Sheets BUS04 and BUS05.

The shire areas have consistently earned the highest operating margins throughout the period, though they fell back from the highs of over 20% seen at the beginning of the period, before falling into the red in the post-pandemic period. Total revenue fell in real terms by almost £775 million a year (27%), whilst costs fell by just £168m (7.4%).

Table C: Local Bus Service Earnings, 2010-2023, English Shires
£m, Constant (June 2023) Prices

Year to 31 March	Total Income	Operating Costs	Surplus/ (Deficit)	Margin (%)
2010	2,879.2	2,278.9	600.3	20.8%
2011	2,836.9	2,243.5	593.4	20.9%
2012	2,791.9	2,312.5	479.4	17.2%
2013	2,731.8	2,282.2	449.6	16.5%
2014	2,735.2	2,297.2	438.0	16.0%
2015	2,689.8	2,269.8	420.0	15.6%
2016	2,602.5	2,295.4	307.0	11.8%
2017	2,583.4	2,245.4	338.0	13.1%
2018	2,561.9	2,154.5	407.3	15.9%
2019	2,536.1	2,167.8	368.3	14.5%
2020	2,441.3	2,046.1	395.2	16.2%
2021	2,211.0	1,924.0	287.1	13.0%
2022	2,081.2	2,131.0	(49.8)	(2.4%)
2023	2,105.4	2,111.0	(5.6)	(0.3%)

5. Scotland

The figures for Scotland are also sourced from DfT statistics provided in Sheets BUS04 and more detailed public spending statistics provided by the Scottish Government.

In contrast the two English areas, both revenue and costs fell in real terms over the period, with £109m less revenue (12.7% down), whilst costs fell by £77m (10.3%). Margins started around 12% but fell back between 2012 and 2015 before recovering to previous levels in the run up to Covid. Since then, two years of losses have been recorded alongside two years of surplus. Fiscal year 2022/23 saw the final year of post-Covid support from the Scottish Government (worth £92m) and the first few months of the Under 22s Concession, which is believed to have boosted patronage.

Table D: Local Bus Service Earnings, 2010-2023, Scotland
£m, Constant (June 2023) Prices

Year to 31 March	Total Income	Operating Costs	Surplus/ (Deficit)	Margin (%)
2010	857.5	750.9	106.6	12.4%
2011	817.2	715.4	101.9	12.5%
2012	819.8	771.0	48.8	6.0%
2013	837.0	744.9	92.1	11.0%
2014	816.5	740.6	75.9	9.3%
2015	794.6	735.6	59.0	7.4%
2016	824.8	723.9	101.0	12.2%
2017	830.1	729.9	100.2	12.1%
2018	805.0	706.5	98.5	12.2%
2019	770.5	768.0	2.5	0.3%
2020	736.6	834.9	(98.3)	(13.3%)
2021	657.5	611.1	46.4	7.1%
2022	643.0	707.5	(64.5)	(10.0%)
2023	748.4	673.8	74.5	10.0%

6. Wales

The figures for Wales are also sourced from DfT statistics provided in Sheets BUS04 and others researched from the Welsh Government's statistical service, States Wales. Looking at figures for operating costs in Wales, there seems to be an understatement when comparing them with other available data from operator statutory accounts and other sources. These show cost levels more closely aligned to those for the English Shire areas.

In order to provide some consistency with the rest of the country, the figures used in the table below have therefore been estimated, using the English Shire per kilometre rates for 70% of the market (our estimate of the mileage operated by the major groups and municipal operations), and the lower rate quoted by DfT for the remainder, operated by local independent operators.

Over the period, operator income fell by £76m (28%) a year in real terms, whilst costs fell by £40m a year (16.5%). As with other areas of the UK, we estimate that losses have been incurred in two of the three years since Covid.

Table D: Local Bus Service Earnings, 2010-2023, Wales
£m, Constant (June 2023) Prices

Year to 31 March	Total Income	Operating Costs	Surplus/ (Deficit)	Margin (%)
2010	237.4	213.5	23.9	10.1%
2011	247.6	216.2	31.4	12.7%
2012	250.9	229.6	21.3	8.5%
2013	258.4	236.0	22.4	8.7%
2014	267.3	244.1	23.3	8.7%
2015	272.0	242.2	29.7	10.9%
2016	272.2	238.5	33.8	12.4%
2017	273.6	240.8	32.8	12.0%
2018	262.7	241.0	21.7	8.3%
2019	235.5	236.5	(0.9)	(0.4%)
2020	228.0	223.3	4.7	2.1%
2021	226.3	230.8	(4.5)	(2.0%)
2022	209.4	209.4	0.1	0.0%
2023	207.4	225.3	(17.9)	(8.6%)

www.ingramcontent.com/pod-product-compliance
Lightning Source LLC
Chambersburg PA
CBHW042019090526
44590CB00029B/4332